*T*he *M*aking of *Y*ou

By

Reverend Michele Taylor

The places, events and situations are real. This is not a fictional story. However, names have been eliminated to protect the people referenced.

ISBN: 1-4107-2441-7 (e-book)
ISBN: 1-4107-2442-5 (Paperback)

Library of Congress Control Number: 2003093892

This book is printed on acid free paper.

Printed in the United States of America
Bloomington, IN

Taylor House Publications
A Division of Taylor Ministries
E-mail: taylorhousepub@hotmail.com

Editorial services: Possibilities Publishing
E-mail: linkstobusiness2@aol.com
Published by 1st Books Library

1stBooks – rev. 05/28/03

Scripture reference:

The Holy Bible King James Version, and the New International Version were indicated

Acknowledgements

I am eternally grateful to the Lord, my God, for looking upon my soul with mercy and compassion. Through His Son, Jesus Christ, I have been redeemed. By His Holy Spirit, I am empowered to do the work for which He has called me to do. (Lord, I lift your name on high— on the wings of my praise.)

A heart full of thanks to my dear friends and family who have labored long with me during the process of my being molded, shaped and refined by God. Your patience and longsuffering was not in vain. (God is not through with me yet.)

To my darling husband, Reverend John W. Taylor, Jr., thank you for loving me through this journey. You know the time and effort that went into this labor of love for the sake of God's people. You prayed me through, endured my early morning and late night rendezvous with the computer and continued to encourage me every step of the way. I appreciate your submission to God's *will* as I pressed forward to complete The Making of You. (Thank God for the unity of the spirit, and our shared vision for the ministry.)

Love to my sister, Justine, who as a personal witness to many of the testimonies shared in this book, extended her unconditional love and prayers while I was yet in the firery furnace of refinement. Thank you for our Saturday morning talks and encouraging me to write. (Through the storms; peace be still.)

Abundant blessings to the Sisterhood: Sarah, Pauleta, Sharon, Samantha and Sabrina, for your friendship, love and support. To Moneick, my dear friend and editor, thank you for your literary expertise and keeping me focused. (To God be the glory.)

To my pastor, Rev. Dr. Del P. Shields, no books could have taught me what I learned under your tutelage. Thank you for the constant push to do better. To my church family (Zion Gospel Church Ministries), I appreciate your love and encouragement. Always endeavor to fulfill your potential and your destiny. God Bless you!

DEDICATION

To the memory of my parents:
Thelma (1963) and Alexander Jackson (1991)
and my stepmother, Rosemary Jackson (2001)
To the many Christians who experienced
"Church Hurt"
or stepped away from the Faith and came back
or want to come back to the Lord.

To everyone who desires to accept Jesus Christ
as your personal Savior, but don't believe
the church-life is for you.

To the Beloved of the Lord who are yet growing
in grace unto spiritual maturity.

Table of Contents

Forward

The Making of You is a labor of love. Reverend Michele Taylor shares with us some of her deepest thoughts and trying experiences as she has worked through her Christian walk with the Lord.

Reverend Taylor has drawn a strength from the Word of God as she shares how we, as Christian Believers, need to grow in our walk with the Savior, Jesus Christ. She even poses many questions to us as to where the Lord is leading us and where we need to look within ourselves to have that closer relationship with the Lord.

Reverend Taylor does not pull punches as to what she is thinking, or how she has come to the conclusions around her experiences. She gets real with us and forces us to get real with ourselves, real in our thoughts, real in our judgments and real with the Lord.

Whether you are a new Christian or one that is seasoned in the Lord or maybe someone who is finding your way, you will find that The Making of You will draw you into a deeper understanding of what the Christian walk requires, and what that deeper relationship with God will mean to you personally.

I encourage you to get your paper and pen and sit with Reverend Taylor as she takes you on a journey towards Christian maturity through Christ Jesus in The Making of You.

Moneick T. Hancock, MS
The Possibilities Group, Founder

Reflections of What I Heard: Preface

God has anointed Reverend Taylor to tell this Truth. A Truth that says let's be real; let's be honest with ourselves first, and then with each other. Expose your "IT" (whatever your "IT" is) and allow healing to take place.

In the sometimes stoic world of Christianity, many Saints walk, talk embrace and act out what they perceive or assume to be their assigned roles in the church as a member of the Body of Christ. Sadly, however, in many instances, God is neither the Producer nor the Director of their "Christian-life Show." Thus, the struggle begins.

This work encouraged me to embrace and praise the Lord for the imperfections that have helped me to be who I am. When I am in the presence of the Lord, I feel complete. However, as I go through the daily functions that form the threads of my life, sometimes I feel flawed. There have been, and continue to be, situations that are not pleasant for me to remember or to deal with. Sometimes I hurt, and I go to God because He can make every situation right. Yet, occasionally I would also like to go to a brother or sister in Christ, or even the leaders of my assembly, and reveal the deeply hidden and hurting inner me. Once, I approached a fellow Saint and slowly began to remove my mask. She also made contact with the image that she was projecting. As a portion of the hidden me was being revealed, I realized that my anticipated confidant was only securing *her* mask. I, in turn, tucked my issues back into myself and felt righteous condemnation for my attempts to tarnish the fellowship of the Saints of God with my imperfections.

As you gaze into the words that God has given Reverend Taylor to share with us, look for your reflection. See yourself as you really are. Allow this work, The Making of You, to minister to your heart and soul. As I read each page, I heard, "You are not alone. You are not crazy. Remove your mask. Lift the curtains; lift your veil, be real and be free in Christ!"

Respectfully submitted by Samantha Williams
The Sisterhood

Introduction

"In Him we were also chosen, having been predestined according to the plan of Him who works out everything in conformity with the purpose of His will, in order that we, who were the first to hope in Christ, might be for the praise of His glory. And you also were included in Christ when you heard the word of truth, the gospel of your salvation. Having believed, you were marked in Him with a seal, the promised Holy Spirit, who is a deposit guaranteeing our inheritance until the redemption of those who are God's possession – to the praise of His glory" (Ephesians 1: 11-14, NIV).

Before there was a "when" and a "where," God knew you. Every aspect of your life was preordained: The good, the bad, the ugly and the indifferent. God deemed it to be so—according to His divine plan—for the purpose of His own glory. Your life has meaning, purpose, value and worth to God! You were chosen to fulfill a destiny that glorifies God and reveals His awesome wonders in the relationship between the Creator and the Created.

We are wonderfully and marvelously made. The Lord carefully sculpts us unto perfection, and He perfects the things concerning us. While the process is often a difficult one wherein we endure many hardships, God's hands mold and shape us into vessels that carry forth the Word of salvation, healing, deliverance and comfort. Yet, it is in the fire that we are refined so that we can do the job that He assigns us to do with strength and fortitude. Herein, our lives are not our own. God has the right to do with us as He pleases, and it pleases Him to fulfill His *will* in us for His glory.

As a young Christian, I was zealous and anxious. I believed that once I gave my life to Christ and received the gift of the Holy Spirit, everything would be just fine. I thought I was on easy street and would enjoy a trouble-free and carefree life in the church. Much to my surprise (and maybe even disbelief), I quickly faced many adversities that no one warned me about when I first got "saved."

Though our destiny is preordained, much of what happens along the way is a direct result of our own decisions. Some of the hardships I faced as a young Christian, I caused myself. Other hardships were inflicted because of who I am in God and what God was shaping me to become. Over the years, I've gone through many situations that helped me to grow spiritually. Every situation I encountered, God used it for my good, and His glory. In the process, I learned to accept the responsibility for my own actions, as well as to endure persecution for righteousness sake. I learned that the details of my life were purposed for the testimony of who God is and what He can do in and through us when we surrender to His *will*. I learned to surrender to God's *will* for my life.

In *The Making of You*, I explore the process of how God shapes our lives as we move towards fulfilling our destiny. Through the development of our spiritual gifts, the turning points in our lives when we've considered suicide, being talked about and betrayed by our Christian brethren, yielding to temptation, falling away from our faith, learning to overcome obstacles and walk in victory, exploring the call to ministry and obeying God, we can grow into Christian maturity. Yet, as long as we choose to follow Christ, we will be confronted by the adversary and challenged to stand tall in our faith. Nevertheless, we have victory in Jesus.

The experiences and testimonies I share with you in *The Making of You* are true. The names have been eliminated to protect the innocent, and the guilty. I pray that you will receive a blessing through the shared word. I pray that you will choose Christ, and trust Him to do a work in you. God is still making you into the vessel He wants to use to draw men and women unto salvation.

As the Lord directs your path and fortifies you through His Word and your Christian experience, He is perfecting you for an effective witness in the Body of Christ. Allow Him to have His way in your life and mold you according to His divine *will* and purpose.

One

TO BE YOUNG AND GIFTED
(The Gift, The Giver and The Deceiver)

"For the gifts and calling of God are without repentance" (Romans 11:29).

SPIRITUAL ENDOWMENT

God breathed, and man became a living soul. With one breath, God deposited into mankind His *charisma* (spiritual endowment, a divine gratuity, deliverance from danger or passion). He freely gave to mankind a portion of His own spirit as an unmerited gift to warn us against the presence of danger, to deliver us from the evils of this world and to guard our soul from the lustful passions of our own carnal mind.

God's breath (His spirit) and charisma (divine gifts)within us warns us of the potential evil we may encounter until such time when we consciously and willfully make a decision to accept Jesus Christ as our Savior. When we accept Jesus into our heart and receive God's *pneuma*

1

(the Holy Spirit internalized), we are filled with the ability to operate in the spirit and to utilize the spiritual gifts that lie dormant within us.

Joel declared in prophecy, *"and it shall come to pass afterward, that I will pour out my spirit upon all flesh; and your sons and daughters shall prophesy, your old men shall dream dreams, and your young men shall see visions" (Joel 2:28).* The prophecy was fulfilled on the day of Pentecost when the Holy Spirit was poured out upon all flesh to be received by those who believe in Jesus Christ as the resurrected Savior. This promise is to all generations. Everyone who is filled with the Holy Spirit is endowed with the power of God that activates the operation of our spiritual gifts.

GIFTED BY NATURE

God breathed into man, and man received the creativity of God that enables us to fulfill our human potential and spiritual destiny. We did nothing to merit spiritual endowment from the Lord. Our spiritual gifts are inherent. They exist within us because God breathed them into us. Therefore, it is important to understand that we are endowed with spiritual gifts without having repentance. *"For the gifts and calling of God are without repentance" (Romans 11:29).* God did not require man to repent at creation in order to receive His divine gratuity. It was only after the fall of man that repentance was required. Prior to the fall, repentance was not necessary. We are spiritually gifted by nature of our human inheritance, not by our desire to be godly sorry.

The devil knows that we are endowed with spiritual gifts, and he knows that we don't know what our spiritual gifts are until they begin to manifest themselves. He also knows that because spiritual gifts are given without repentance, he can manipulate them at will until we repent. Our free choice, our decision to choose Christ over the devil, determines what spiritual influence we adhere to. Only by repentance, the acceptance of Jesus Christ as our personal Savior and the infilling of the Holy Spirit can spiritual gifts be activated and used for Godly purposes. If our spiritual gifts are exposed to influences that reject God, they can be corrupted for the purpose of ungodly use by demonic forces.

Once our spiritual gifts are activated, whether by the Holy Spirit or by demonic influence, we can see their manifestation in more pronounced ways. As our spiritual gifts begin to emerge, they need to be nurtured, cared for, protected and constantly inspired so that they can reach their full potential and maturation. Who is caring for your spiritual gifts—God, or the devil? Who is guiding the use of your spiritual gifts—the Holy Spirit, or a demonic influence?

BEDAZZLED

Satan draws on man's innate desire to embrace spiritual awareness. He bedazzles our mind with the enticements of pseudo-enlightenment and insight into the supernatural realm. Then he takes advantage of our inherited sinful nature and tricks us into believing that we are the source of our own power, and that the power which ignites our spiritual gifts comes from our own *will*. Many are tricked to believe that God is not the giver of our spiritual gifts, and the Holy Spirit is not the power that activates our gifts. This concept implies that since we are created in the image of God, like God, we are a self-contained power and can delve into the spirit world at will. We can tangibly create anything that the mind can conceive, and we can be our own god.

To impart such deception into the minds and hearts of children is a Satanic strategy that has and continues to influence the direction of many of our children—even into adulthood. We who are given the task of caretaker, or watchman over the souls of our children must understand the seriousness of the task. We cannot be ignorant to Satan's tactics to steal, kill, distort and destroy their God-given spiritual gifts. It is our duty to watch as well as pray so that we can recognize the destroyer when he comes, intercede for our children and help them to realize the purpose and potential of their spiritual gifts and talents.

SPIRITUAL GIFTS IN CHILDREN

When we look into the eyes of our children, we can see their innocence, strengths and challenges. Their spiritual gifts are raw, uncontaminated and untouched by man's self-willed nature, greed and insatiable appetite for power and control. As they grow, we can see their natural abilities imparted by divine breath, and their spiritual gifts beginning to emerge. They themselves may not know or understand their gifts (the essence of the Holy Spirit enveloping their lives) or the magnitude of their inner abilities. Yet they are open and susceptible to the external and internal forces that influence the development and fulfillment of their human potential and spiritual gifts.

The same way in which we can see our children's potential and recognize their spiritual gifts, Satan sees them as well. From the day of

5

conception, he devises a plan to destroy the gifts within. The first line of attack is an attempt to kill the child. If the devil can physically kill the child, the gift that might be used to change the world or expose the devil for who he is will also be destroyed. Consider the birth of Jesus Christ—the gift of redemption to humankind. When Herod learned of the birth of Jesus, he sent three wise men (The Three Kings) to find baby Jesus and to tell him of the child's whereabouts. Herod pretended to want to worship the child, but in reality his intent was to kill Him. The three kings were instructed by God through a dream not to return to Herod to give him the news. During the same time, Joseph was instructed in a dream to take his family to Egypt.

When Herod received word that the three kings returned to their own country, he became furious and commanded that all children two years of age and under living in Bethlehem and neighboring towns be killed. Jesus and His parents remained safe in Egypt until the death of Herod. Had Herod found and killed baby Jesus, Satan would have successfully killed God's gift of salvation to mankind; a gift He freely gave. If Satan can activate such a vicious plot against our Lord Jesus Christ, he will do the same to us. He will try to destroy any child that is destined to serve God and carry the good news of salvation and deliverance.

When Satan cannot kill our children(and their gifts), he tries to corrupt them in their childhood in order to influence the use of their spiritual gifts before they are recognized, nurtured and matured. He becomes a pretender—an imitator of God—and distorts that good and perfect gift within them while they are young in age, tender in heart and innocent in spirit. If Satan can capture our children's spirit by capturing their mind, he can temporarily control the direction of their destiny. (I use the term "temporarily" because when we are chosen by God, our ultimate destiny is to fulfill His *will*. There will come a time when we are all given a choice to serve God or Satan. Regardless of Satan's influence, the stronghold can be broken, and God's *will* will be done. Satan's hold is temporary and only by God's permission.)

THIS IS PERSONAL

Many of you have a story to tell about how the devil tried to kill you as a child. This reality is very personal to me because I know Satan tried to kill me while I was yet in my mother's womb. My mother was diagnosed with breast cancer and was told to terminate the fetus so that she could live. She was told that one of us, if not both of us

7

(she or me) would die if she carried the pregnancy to full term. She was a Godly woman and put her trust in the Lord. Against the doctor's recommendations, she carried me to full term. I'm told that she nearly died giving birth to me.

The Lord kept my mother and allowed her to live two more years before the cancer consumed her body. I believe that had she lost faith and given up on God's ability to keep her during the pregnancy, I would not be here today. I know in my heart that she talked to the Lord about what would become of her child after her death. I also believe that she dedicated my life to the service of the Lord while I was yet in her womb.

Due to my mother's illness during her pregnancy with me, I was born a sickly child and remained so most of my childhood years. The slightest cold turned into bronchitis, and a simple nose-bleed became a fountain of blood. Satan tried to kill me before birth, after birth and throughout my young life in order to keep the gifts of God from developing within me, but God kept me from death because He intended to use my life for kingdom building. Praise the Lord!

DREAMS AND VISIONS

One of the first manifestations of spiritual gifts in children comes in the form of dreams and visions. My earliest memory of having a spiritual gift is when I was three years of age. I didn't know I had a gift, and I certainly didn't understand its potential. As far as I was concerned, I had a bad dream! I dreamed that my god-brother, who while serving in the US Army and was stationed in Viet Nam at the time, was blown up. I clearly saw him step on something and fly into the air from the explosion. I cried so hysterically that my whole family was awakened. I couldn't stop crying because it seemed so real. Not long after having the dream, my god-mother took me to the Veteran's Hospital to visit my god-brother. What I thought was a bad dream turned out to be a vision. I can remember that many of my dreams came true. I spent a good portion of my childhood being afraid to sleep because I didn't want to dream. I was particularly afraid of dreams where I was being chased by huge dark men. Children often have nightmares about being chased. (You may remember a few yourself.) Most often, we as adults "pay them no mind." However, my own experience has taught me to pay close attention to children when they talk about their dreams and nightmares. Especially the ones that involve being chased by monsters. Although we know that movie characters like Freddy Krueger are merely actors in costumes and theatrical makeup, the concept of a demonized creature who enters a child's dream and goes on a killing rampage is steeped in something real and concrete in the spirit world.

I've come to understand that demonic forces can enter into our sleep and snatch the life right out of us. Many of us are attacked in our sleep as adults and struggle to overcome the demonic forces, or recuperate from the attack. Can you imagine how much more difficult is it for children who don't understand the attack and don't know how to fight off the attack? Not only is the experience of being attacked by the devil in one's sleep frightening and traumatic, it is also paralyzing.

The fear placed in the heart of children from demonic activity that occurs in their sleep stays in their subconscious mind. When the memory is triggered again in adulthood, it reproduces the same physical and emotional response to fear as it did during childhood. If the cycle of fear is not broken, they will experience the same trauma and paralyzing feeling when they become an adult as they did when they were young. Therefore, I admonish you to pay close attention when your child tells you about a bad dream or vision. Listen carefully and ask God for discernment and direction. It is important for you to guide your child through this experience so that they can break through the fear factor and arm themselves with the weapons of spiritual warfare.

FASCINATION WITH THE SUPERNATURAL

My spiritual gifts were in operation very early in my life even though I had not yet repented and accepted Jesus Christ as my personal Savior. I knew there was a God, but I did not seek salvation. Rather, I chose to explore the supernatural. Like Joseph, the prince of Egypt, I was able to interpret dreams at a very young age. If someone told me their dream, I interpreted it. I could see into the spirit realm and communicate with familiar spirits. I was able to predict events before they happened, and if I said something would happen, it did. If I had a headache, I "willed it away." If someone was in pain, I absorbed their pain to myself and released it simply by exerting mind power. If a teacher said, "turn to page 73," I turned directly to page 73. What was frightening (as I reflect) is that I enjoyed having the ability to do the extraordinary.

I realized that there was a power within me, but I didn't understand this power or the complexity of Satan's deceptions in using it. When my spirit was opened to receive the supernatural, I tried to embrace it. The more I used my gifts, the sharper the gifts became. Misguided by Satan's hand, I persistently pursued to know the unknown. It was my attempt to overcome the fear of seeing demons when I walked down the street, or looked into someone's eyes. I began to read books on the supernatural and paranormal not realizing how the devil was drawing me into his trap and attempting to turn me away from God before I could repent and accept salvation.

I was intrigued by astrology and how it explained people's character. I indulged in meditation, and I encountered an out-of-body experience on many occasions. I also tampered with self-hypnosis and the concept of reincarnation. As a result of my tampering, I began to experience a psychic phenomena and the supernatural like never before. The more willing I was to explore this venue of supernatural communication, the more susceptible I became to demonic influence.

As with myself, it is common for the young and gifted to be fascinated by the supernatural.

The young are often drawn to an unknown power by a supernatural power that promises to give them eternal power. Youth have in so many ways been denied personal power that they tend to seek it in whatever form they can. On the positive side, some join peer mediation groups wherein their gifts and strengths are acknowledged by their ability to prevent other youth from fighting or getting involved in deviant and self-destructive behavior. Others engage in some type of church-related activity or community recreational program. On the negative side, some engage in gang activities wherein their manhood or womanhood is said to be proven when they take another person's life.

Then there's another group that chooses to join a cult (or the occult) to separate themselves from society and explore the power within. Their exploration often leads to deeper levels of Satanic experimentation wherein they are no longer in control of their actions. They become receptacles and conduits for the transferring and infiltration of demonic spirits. They're playing with fire when they sell their souls to the devil—consciously or unconsciously—for the promise of an unlimited power that they will never fully achieve. This deception will take them straight to Hell.

PLAYING WITH FIRE

Any tampering with Satan and his empts is a dangerous game. As the old adage says, "When you play with fire, you will surely get burned." Fire is fire. No matter how small the flame, it will burn you and cause excruciating pain if you continue to tamper with it. I experimented with the supernatural during my early years and into my teen years. Some of my experiences were innocent child's play at the time, while others were intentional and led to delving more deeply into Satan's den. Nevertheless, God used every situation I was exposed to as part of the process of molding and shaping me into a vessel that could be used for His purpose.

I remember as a child that my teenage sisters had friends who often tampered with the supernatural by playing with the Ouija Board and conducting seances. They told stories about conjuring up spirits, candles going out and books flying off the sink into a bathtub filled with water. They spoke about specific spirits by name that came back through seances and lived in the house. One day, one of my sisters and I wanted to see for ourselves if there was any truth to this Ouija Board. So we tried it out. I don't recall any spirits that came through, but I remember us fighting about who was moving the indicator and who blew out the candle. Every time we played with the game, we encountered a different experience that left us wondering...is it just a game?

Our fascination with the supernatural even took us on a ghost-hunting adventure. Supposedly, our older sister's friend lived in a haunted house. This friend had younger sisters the same age as my sister and I. One day we all decided to check out the ghosts in the basement, just for the fun of it. We could not have imagined what we were in for. When we opened the closet door in the basement, nothing was there, just blackness. We laughed at ourselves and began to close the closet door when an old woman appeared and moved towards us. We were out of there! We were petrified! When we got upstairs to where the teens were hanging out, not one of us said a word to the other. We basically just stared into space catching a glimpse of each other's eyes. That was the last time my sister and I went into that house.

That experience should have been the end of my search to know the unknown, but it wasn't. My curiosity lured me deeper into Satan's den. I was entranced, hooked. I wanted to know more. In junior high school, one of my classmates told us that her house was haunted. A group of us went there during lunch to see what was going on. We performed an impromptu seance.

Suddenly, there were strange noises in the house, things fell and the kitchen cabinet doors opened and slammed closed. (I saw this with my own eyes.) We hauled out of there with a quickness!

Back at school, we shared this experience with a science teacher and questioned the existence of the supernatural. He willingly engaged in the discussion. Other classmates also sought answers about the paranormal. As a scientific experiment, we conducted a seance to call back the spirit of Dr. Martin Luther King, Jr. Of course, Dr. King did not appear! However, there was definitely a strange presence in the classroom. The sound of a fallen textbook hitting the floor broke the silence. I don't know what we called up, but something came through.

At the time, I did not know that spiritual gifts come without repentance. I knew about the spirit realm and spiritual gifts, but repentance was not yet a factor in the equation. Yes, I believed in God, but I wasn't saved. Therefore, I had not submitted the use of the gifts back to the gift-giver. I thought that since I wasn't using my gifts for evil, there was no problem. I found comfort in elevating my spirit outside of my body and transcending my psychic mind into the supernatural realm. There, beyond my consciousness, I found no pain.

I believe that my experimentation with the supernatural opened the portholes for demonic

16

infiltration, and I had become a conduit for demonic service unawares. Satan was subtle in his deception and convinced me that by obtaining knowledge and tampering with the supernatural world, I had a form of God's power within me. In reality, I had denied God as the source of the power and took on the powers of a pseudo god. Misguided and misdirected, I had become a puppet to Satan's whimsy. Under his influence, I played with the fire of witchcraft, and I got burnt.

Satan laughed at God because he thought he caught my soul hook, line and sinker. But God, in His infinite mercy, planned the day of salvation before the very foundation of the earth was lain. My salvation was promised from generation to generation as far back as Calvary. Jesus died for my sake and bought my soul with the price of His own life. However, salvation had to be my choice. In due season, I chose to repent and give my life to Christ. I chose to surrender my heart and return the use of my spiritual gifts back to God (the giver of the gifts).

Many Christians have had experiences with the supernatural at a young age. Because these experiences do not exemplify Christ, they choose not to talk about them. In part, they are embarrassed and afraid to share their testimony of God's deliverance. I, too, felt embarrassed. However, I now know that God intended to use my testimony to deliver someone else, and to

17

help others understand the subtlety with which Satan influences our children to misuse their spiritual gifts. My hope is that through the experiences I've shared with you concerning my own encounters with demonic influence at a young age, you have seen how easy it is for the young and gifted to be trapped by evil when it is disguised in such delectable packages as "acceptance and power."

I pray that you are encouraged to release your own testimony. Though it is not an easy thing to do, someone needs to hear your testimony so that they can gain hope for their own deliverance. Not only will your testimony bless someone else, the weight of the secret fault you carried for so many years will be lifted. What a blessed assurance we have in knowing that Jesus saves and delivers. (Hallelujah.) He saved my soul and delivered me from witchcraft because I wanted to be saved! He will save you, too, (and your children) if you want to be saved; and He will deliver you from the sin of witchcraft, if you want to be delivered.

DELIVERANCE IS MINE

I know the Lord preordained my exposure to the supernatural at a young age as an important factor in the process of molding me for godly purposes. As the potter with his clay, God's hands were upon me shaping and reshaping me for His divine use. The Lord conditioned me and prepared me to take a stand against evil. This is my testimony.

At the age of 19, I dated a young man with whom I was deeply in love. In fact, we previously dated in our early teens. Somehow, our paths crossed again, and we picked up where we left off. His mother worked at a night club, and one night he brought me there to introduce us. She looked at me, leaned over the bar and said, "You have a powerful gift. If you don't use it, you will lose it." I was stunned by her directness, but I knew what she was talking about.

Throughout the relationship, my boyfriend and I seemed to be so in tuned with each other that we knew each other's thoughts before we would speak. He often called me just at the moments I thought about calling him. I would hear his voice in my mind telling me to meet him at a specific location and time, and I would. One day, I envisioned him getting shot. Sure enough, he called me from the hospital to let me know that he had been shot in the leg.

The relationship between his mother and I continued to develop. We spent a lot of time talking, watching television, drinking herbal tea and reading tarot cards. The more interest I showed in the tarot cards, the more she talked with me about the supernatural, spiritual abilities and using "the gift." As time went on, she revealed her true self. One day, she openly shared that she worshipped Satan, and then proceeded to show me her altar. She described herself as a high priestess. When I talked with my boyfriend about what his mother shared with me, he politely showed me a medallion he wore around his neck and asked me if I knew what it meant. I didn't know, so he told me that it meant he, too, was a devil worshipper.

The wall that connected my boyfriend's apartment to his mother's apartment was the same wall where her worship altar was placed. One night, I awakened to a strange sound that startled me. I was alone and thought my boyfriend was coming into the apartment. I tried to get up, but my body was sluggish. When I pulled myself up and realized that it was not my boyfriend, I forced myself to get off the bed and turn the light on, but I couldn't find the light switch. I tried to make my way to the bathroom in the dark. When I walked through the kitchen to get to the bathroom, the wall connecting my boyfriend's apartment with his mother's apartment wasn't there. It was as if the two rooms had become one. In the blackness, I saw his mother's altar with candles burning. The gates of Hell were wide open. (Eternal damnation was knocking hard.) Not believing what I saw, I kept feeling my way to the bathroom and turned on the light. The next day, his mother told me she saw me when I went to the bathroom. Then she asked me what I saw. When I told her, she reminded me about "the gift" and asked me what I was going to do with it.

My spiritual senses were awakened in a way that I cannot explain. I saw the demons as they raced through the apartment, and I came to know their presence immediately. On one occasion, my boyfriend and I were intimately engaged; and in the height of the moment, I saw his body transform into some kind of demon. I tried to push him off of me and re-focus my eyes. Then the figure disappeared. A little more than a month after that experience, I dreamed that his mother put something into my tea and tried to force me to drink it. She said that the baby I was carrying belonged to Satan and required special care. In the dream, I knocked the cup of tea out of her hand and told her that I would never bear Satan's child. I promised her that if the baby did not belong to God, I would kill it, and I began to pray in the dream. Whatever it was that I prayed must have touched the heart of God. A week after the dream, I started to bleed unusually heavily. I went to the doctor and learned that I had a miscarriage. Like many of my dreams, this one came true, too.

What I didn't understand at the time was that God had a different plan for my life. I didn't understand the spiritual warfare I was engaged in, or how it would effect my life today. What I now know is that God was merciful, even when I didn't understand His "mercy." The Lord dealt with me intensely in dreams and visions. God showed me what I had gotten myself into. Several dreams revealed detailed events that included people's names, cars and license plate numbers. I shared the details of one particular dream with my boyfriend, and he filled in the details as I spoke confirming that everything I dreamed was real. God even allowed me to see the details of my own death if I chose to stay in that relationship.

The Lord knocked on the door of my heart many times, but I was so entranced (and so in love) that I couldn't break from the yoke of bondage. The saving grace (and it was grace that saved me) was in knowing that "God Is!" Because God had a plan for my life, He mercifully delivered me out of the hands of the enemy. I loved this man so much that I almost lost my soul because of him. Then God pulled the blinders from my eyes. I can truly say that I once was blind and now I see.

As the Lord whispered to my heart, the devil tried another strategy to bind me, but his true intent was revealed. My boyfriend decided that it was time for us to get married. He told me all the things he was involved in; selling and transporting drugs, prostitution, and the black mafia. He felt that if we were going to be together, I needed to know about the "empire." He revealed that someone was watching my every move. He knew who my friends were, what I did and when, where I went, who I talked to, and so much more. He told me that the life I knew was over, and I had to die to it in order to live with him. In his own way, he attempted to show me the kingdom I could rule if I would just bow down and worship Satan.

Devastated by the unveiling, I stopped associating with all of my friends. I isolated myself and turned away from my family because I was afraid something would happen to them. I disengaged myself from everything and everyone. I was afraid to tell anyone because I didn't feel they would believe me or understand. I was so afraid that I wanted to kill myself. (Why wouldn't God let me die?) Then a gentle voice said, "PRAY." Pray? How could I pray? Would God hear me? Would He forgive my abominations? I didn't know, but I prayed anyway. Surely, if God was merciful, He would hear my pitiful, sorrowful and desperate cry for help.

My boyfriend was contracted to kill someone in Puerto Rico. In the sanctuary of my heart and the solitude of my bedroom, I cried unto the Lord. "Lord, I'm sorry. Forgive me. Help me Jesus." I cried so much that night, I can't even tell you the words I uttered to the Father. This I do know, I prayed to God like never before. I told God that if He brought my boyfriend home without killing whoever it was he was supposed to kill, and if He got me out of that mess, I would serve Him. I told Him, "God if it means I have to quit him (my boyfriend) and give my life to you (the Lord), I will." When my boyfriend came home, he told me he didn't do the job. Something happened, and he didn't have to go through with it. I didn't know if he was lying or telling the truth, but he said what I wanted to hear. Then he told me that he wanted to get married right away because he felt that he was losing me. There was no way I was going to elope! The way of escape was provided, and I told him no because I wanted my family to be there.

When I left his house that day in October, 1979, my whole life changed. I began to pray more, and I found the strength to resist the lure of Satan's folly. I never returned to that apartment again. I didn't answer his phone calls, and I prayed him out of my mind when his face appeared in dreams and visions. I consciously decided that I didn't want to serve Satan. I wanted God in my life, not the devil! In December, I gave my life to Christ. I repented, I was baptized and I received the infilling of the Holy Spirit. (Thank you Jesus.)

The spiritual gifts became more pronounced once they were activated by the Holy Spirit. The same way I dreamed dreams and had visions when I wasn't saved, I dreamed even more. Not long after I accepted Christ in my life, I dreamed that I was walking my dog, and a car pulled up beside me. A man got out of the car and handed me a brown envelope. He told me to forget I ever knew (what's his name), and that what was in the envelope would compensate me for all the trouble. The man told me that (what's his name) was dead, and he wanted me to be taken care of. When I looked in the envelope, I saw bundles of money. It was a payoff to keep me from telling what I knew.

One day, I saw that man in his car. Driving slowly, he looked at me with a rather devious smile and followed me for about two blocks— though he never got out and handed me an envelope. (Now that I think about it, I believe the dream and the true to life experience was the devil's way of trying to keep me quiet. Perhaps it was a type of payoff to keep me from sharing my testimony. Well, today, I consider it to be a voided contract, because I'm telling on the devil! There's nothing he can offer me to keep my mouth shut!)

I saw my ex-boyfriend a few months after I accepted Christ into my life, and I declared to him my salvation and love for God. He told me that he couldn't deal with me leaving him for another man, but he could handle the fight with God. He attempted to woo me back by appealing to my sensuality and memories of our sexual relationship (something that in times past, I couldn't resist.) That was Satan's way of telling me that the battle was not over. He wanted my soul and was determined to fight for it. The attacks kept coming in different forms. I stepped off the sidewalk curb of a deserted street, and a car nearly hit me. My cat crawled over my neck during my sleep and sat on my windpipe causing me to choke. When I awakened, the cat hissed at me and began to scratch at my face. Satan showed himself to me on a television screen that wasn't even turned on. Oh, the list goes on.

The dreams continued, and the devil invaded my sleep with a host of demons scurrying after my soul. The difference was that I learned how to rebuke him and apply the Blood of Jesus. With every attack by demonic forces, I cried out, "The Blood of Jesus." I learned to say with authority, "Satan, I rebuke you in the name of Jesus. Get thee behind me." (Thank you Lord for your blood that cleanses the sin-sick soul. Thank you Lord for your blood that still washes. Just one drop of your blood washes and cleanses. Thank you Lord for the miraculous power of your blood, and the power and authority in the name of Jesus. Hallelujah!)

FROM ONE EXTREME TO THE NEXT

The first six months of salvation were probably the most critical, in terms of breaking the chains of demonic influence and understanding the acceptance (or lack thereof) of spiritual gifts in the Body of Christ. My pastor told me how to receive full deliverance from the demonic influence of my ex-boyfriend. I took everything my ex-boyfriend gave me over the years, doused them with anointing oil and burned them. I verbally denounced Satan and all affiliation with him. I was free, and I knew I was free. Satan no longer controlled the spiritual gifts within me, and my ex-boyfriend could no longer enter my mind at will. I was delivered.

During a testimony service, I shared my experience with the members. I was so happy about what God had done that I wanted everyone to know. I thought that by sharing my testimony with the believers, they would rejoice with me. Instead of rejoicing, some of the members became obsessed with "casting the devil out." Rumors spread throughout the congregation that I was demon possessed. I felt humiliated and embarrassed. The experience made me question my own deliverance and not want to go back to church.

I was asked to speak with a Bishop from a Church with which we fellowshipped to determine whether or not an "exorcism" was required. The Bishop talked with me and asked several questions about what was going on with me and why I was sent to meet with him. When I explained my story, the Bishop put me into the hands of the missionaries. The missionaries prayed with me seemingly for hours. We prayed and we prayed and we prayed some more until they were satisfied with the manifestation of the Holy Spirit evidenced by the speaking in tongues. After the ordeal, the Bishop called my pastor personally and told him that I was not demon possessed, and to tell the Church members to leave me alone.

This was quite a traumatic experience for a young adult and a new born-again Christian. From one extreme to the next, this experience could have forced me out of the church and back into the hands of the devil, but my heart was fixed on serving God. I promised the Lord that I would serve Him, come what may. Because of that one experience, I suppressed my spiritual gifts, and my testimony. I didn't want to be labeled and cast aside. I believed that the church members would always look at me and wonder if I was every really saved. What I didn't understand was that it was a trick of the devil to convince me that he still had control, and that I was not delivered. The devil attempted to deceive me once again so that the gifts of God would not be used for godly purposes. Once again, he tried to convince me that if I would just bow down and serve him (because the Church rejected me), he would stir up the gifts in me and allow me entrance into the spirit realm. (Oh, to be young, gifted and deceived! Does anyone know what I'm talking about?)

I thank the Lord that my steps are ordered by God. Whether or not I understood the reasons why I had to go through all that I went through as a young and gifted vessel, both in the world and in the Church, I know that God allowed me to experience His mercy every step of the way because my experiences would become my testimony. I know what it is to be young, gifted and deceived; and thanks be to God, I know what it is to be delivered.

MY DEEP CONCERN

Believers need to know about the demonic influence that entrance our children's mind and spirit when they watch certain cartoons, video tapes, music and motion pictures. We need to be aware of the many vehicles used for demonic entrapment. We need to know that demons are speaking to our children whether we choose to believe it or not. The newspapers are filled with captions about school kids killing their classmates because they heard voices in their head telling them to "go and kill." Kids need to know that they don't have to stay in Satanic bondage. They need to know that there's a way out. The way out is Jesus. How will they know if we don't tell them? It is our job to tell them!

It's easy to deceive the young and the gifted when they are eager to be used by God. As adults, we tend to take full advantage of the fact that the young are just that—young. They will do what we tell them to do out of respect because we are adults and have authority over them. (Or, they will rebel.) My own experience lets me know that the young and gifted are often used, abused and misunderstood—even in the Body of Christ. At any given time, the Church Body can either encourage, discourage, exploit or covet the spiritual gifts of the young and gifted. As adults, we are often guilty of causing our youth to believe that what they are doing is to please God, when in reality it is to please us. In doing so, we teach them how to be deceptive, too.

I am deeply concerned about what the church is doing (or not doing) to help the young and gifted to identify, understand and nurture their spiritual gifts. As adults, we have the responsibility of helping to nurture that good and perfect gift that God has placed in our youth. Yet because of our own sins of jealousy, envy, malice, hate, coveting, lust, vanity, pride and great expectations, we ignore our youth, punish them to the point where they don't want to do anything, or we attempt to hold them down so that they don't rise up above us. Often we expect too much too soon, and we are disappointed when they don't live up to our expectations. Or, we ignore the development of their gifts and use them to satisfy our own selfish desires and motives.

Let's not be guilty of helping the devil to kill, steal and destroy the spiritual gifts in our youth. Let us surrender our selfish motives and false expectations for our youth and seek the divine *will* of God for their lives. Before we impose our own desires and expectations of how God will use the spiritual gifts in the youth of our church, ask the question, "What are God's expectations?" God expects all believers of all ages to be holy.

We need to teach our youth to be holy and to seek God's *will* in their lives. Teach them to please God, not the adult who decides whether or not they can sing in the choir, lead the prayer or read the scriptures. Allow the spiritual gifts of God to rise up in our youth in their own season so that they don't become pretenders of the faith. Help the young and gifted to understand that there is a divine plan and a divine purpose for their lives, and that God is making them through a molding and shaping process.

DIVINE PURPOSE

The same spiritual gifts that I was endowed with when God breathed life into my body at birth are the same spiritual gifts He activated in me when I received the baptism of the Holy Spirit. The spiritual gifts that I abused in my youth were not taken away from me. Rather, when I surrendered my life to the Lord, I surrendered Satan's control of the gifts and committed them to God's service. In time, and with much prayer and supplication, I learned that God has a divine purpose for the use of all spiritual gifts. I learned that what the devil tried to steal from me belonged to God, and it is impossible to steal from God without paying a severe consequence. Satan is already condemned to Hell, and he wanted to take me with him. If I did not give my life to Christ, and surrender the use of the spiritual gifts in me back to the Father, my soul would have been condemned to Hell. That's a rather severe consequence for an ounce of false power. The Holy Spirit delivered me from evil, and God gave me a new life in Christ.

Spiritual gifts are disseminated by God with a divine and holy purpose. God expects the gifts to be used according to His divine *will*. The more spiritual gifts God endows you with, the more He expects you to do in the Kingdom. *"For unto whom much is given, of him much is required" (Luke 12:48).* God purposed in me to become a warrior for spiritual warfare in the Body of Christ. One of the gifts the Lord endowed me with (entrusted to my care) is the gift of discernment—the ability to know and see the presence of the supernatural, both demonic and angelic. It is not a gift that I asked for, or desired. However, God graced me with this gift because He purposed to use me in spiritual warfare. (Hallelujah) He knew that my heart belonged to Him and that one day He could trust me to use the gifts according to His *will*. People who are gifted with strong discernment have the potential to effectively pull down strongholds in the church, in their homes, in their family and anywhere God may choose to use them. I am blessed and humbled that God chose me for such a task; and in choosing me, He equipped me through pure experience.

Spiritual gifts are divine, the giver of the gifts is divine and the purpose of the gifts is divine. Spiritual gifts require nurturing, wisdom in their use and the discipline of prayer and fasting. Submit yourself to discipline and sacrifice and deny the lusts of the flesh so that the spirit of God can live in you and teach you all things relevant to the gifts within you. Allow yourself to be taught and nurtured by those who have experience. Remember that the deceiver is always lurking about. You will be under constant attack by demonic forces that want to steal God's glory through the vice of self-glorification and pride, kill your spiritual gifts before they are nurtured and matured, and destroy the good within the gift and turn its use towards evil.

Let God arise in you so that the demons will scatter. Let the Holy Spirit control your spiritual gifts and teach you to use them with reverence and respect towards God. We are wonderfully and marvelously made in the image of God. To be young and gifted is an honor and a privilege. It is also a responsibility. God has bestowed this honor upon us before the foundation of the earth was lain. I pray that we will express our gratitude for such a gratuity. May God continue to be merciful and turn every adverse situation into an opportunity for *the making of you.*

Reflections

1)   Do you remember any childhood experiences that helped you to identify your spiritual gifts?

2)   Do you recall any dreams and visions you had as a child that came true?

3)   Are you hiding your spiritual gifts, or misusing them?

4)   Are you ashamed of your testimony? There's no need for shame. Your testimony is a blessing of deliverance for someone else. Tell it!

This is my prayer

Lord, thou art God. You blessed us from the beginning of time. You knew us before we were conceived, and you knew what you purposed for our lives. You gave to us a part of yourself when we didn't even know you. You placed your spirit within us for a holy and divine purpose. Thank you, Lord, for your graciousness.

I ask you to help us, Father, to understand and accept the spiritual gifts that you have entrusted to our care. Help us to understand how the experiences you've allowed us to have were purposed to nurture and develop our spiritual gifts for Kingdom work. Help us to be mindful not to abuse the gifts in ourselves or in others.

Father, impart in us discernment to know when the gifts are motivated by your Holy Spirit and when they are guided by Satanic influence. Help us to see Satan's deceptions and teach us how to respond appropriately. Bind the spirit of vanity, pride and self-glory within us that seeks to steal your glory.

We submit ourselves to your spirit. We submit ourselves to your *will*. Use us, Lord, according to your divine purpose. Amen.

TWO

TURNING POINTS
(Suicide is Not an Option)

"Hear my prayer, O Lord, and let my cry come unto thee. Hide not thy face from me in the day when I am in trouble; incline thine ear unto me; in the day when I call answer me speedily. For my days are consumed like smoke, and my bones are burned as an hearth. My heart is smitten, and withered like grass; so that I forget to eat my bread. By reason of the voice of my groaning my bones cleave to my skin. I am like a pelican of the wilderness: I am like an owl of the desert. I watch, and am as a sparrow alone upon the house top…My days are like a shadow that declineth; and I am withered like grass" (Psalm 102:1-7, 11).

"Hear my cry, O God; attend unto my prayer. From the end of the earth will I cry unto thee, when my heart is overwhelmed: lead me to the rock that is

higher than I. For thou hast been a shelter for me, and a strong tower from the enemy. I will abide in thy tabernacle forever: I will trust in the covert of thy wings" (Psalm 61:1-4).

CROSSROADS

Every one of us has had to make tough decisions at what seemed to be the most difficult time of our lives. Our decisions, whether made with good or poor judgment, catapulted us into a series of events that caused us to either err from the path of righteousness and our preordained destiny, or to become more determination to go forward and reach our goal. Every decision we made in that crucial moment effected our lives for the rest of our lives. We were at a *crossroad* trying to figure out which way to go without having the understanding that whatever our decision, we were certain to encounter our preordained destiny. Often we found ourselves turning around in a circle frantically trying to capture a glimpse of what was behind us and what's a little further down the road in front of us. If only we could have seen in the distance, we would have known the better way to go. Making decisions is never easy, but the process is necessary for *the making of you.* Whatever our choices, we are guaranteed that the molding and shaping of who we are is directly related to the decisions we've made and will make.

What's difficult about being at *crossroads* is that we don't have a lot of time to think. We can't always just pause and meditate. Usually, there's no one around for us to ask directions or to tell us which way to go. There's no "Map of Life" we can pull out and read before choosing the right road to travel. Most likely, we're in a situation wherein we have to make a quick decision, and then live with it—come what may. Sometimes our gut, or instinct, tells us to go left, but we go right instead. Then we find ourselves in a grand mess that could have been avoided if we had just listened to that inner voice that said, "Go left."

HELPLESSNESS AND HOPELESSNESS

Many of us are at a *crossroad* right now and have to make a very important decision—a decision that will bring life or death. Sometimes circumstances can push us to the edge of helplessness and hopelessness. We can't seem to get the help we need, and that makes us feel hopeless. Without hope, we just want to give up and die. We stand at the *crossroad* knowing that if we walk down the road of hopelessness, we're sure to encounter death. While it appears to be the easier road to travel because we know what the end will be, it can also be the road that leads to the death of our soul—eternally.

On the other side of hopelessness, we encounter the road of uncertainty. We don't know what lies ahead. We don't know what obstacles we'll have to get around, or what deceptions will cause our vision to be obscured. We don't see the victory that awaits us further down the way. To walk down the road of uncertainty is a frightening experience. We have to really exercise our faith that once we start the journey, we'll make it to the other side victoriously. It is a more difficult road to travel, but it's the road that brings life instead of death.

I've been to the *crossroads* of helplessness, hopelessness and uncertainty many times. I lost all hope, and I wanted to give up. I couldn't see a reason for living. My state of helplessness lead me to a condition of hopelessness, and I wanted to take the easy way out. I made a lot of decisions that thrust me on to the road of self-destruction. I can only liken the experience to that of being blind-folded and spun around and around and around. Wherever I stopped, that's the direction I walked in. Every path I took led to another path, which led to another path, which led to another path, and so on. At the end of each path, there was another *crossroad* and more decisions to make. Life had become a never-ending maze of roads that led to self-destruction. Sometimes, it seemed easier to walk down the road of hopelessness and self-destruction than to walk by faith down the road of uncertainty to victory.

THE ROAD TO SELF-DESTRUCTION

When I think about *crossroads*, I think about situations in my life that were filled with so much emotional suffering and inner turmoil, heartache and heartbreak, confusion and disillusion, that all I wanted to do was die. I literally stood on the top of a mountain, leaned over and contemplated the fall. I stood at the edge of a subway platform rocking back and forth hoping I'd lose my balance and fall onto the tracks in front of an on coming train. I pressed the razor blade deep enough into my wrist to draw blood—wanting to make one clean cut across the vein. I took enough pills to put me to sleep forever, so I thought, but woke up just the same. I was standing at the *crossroads* of life and death, and I decided to die. I turned to every self-destructive habit I knew— sex, drugs and alcohol. I didn't care about myself, or the consequences of my recklessness. I just wanted to kill the pain. I lived on the edge of the road of destruction hoping that my decisions would one day take me out of my misery.

Have you ever been in that place where you just wanted to die; where suicide looked like the only way of escape? Have you been to that place where mental anguish and emotional turmoil wrapped themselves so deeply around despair that your soul hungered for death? Circumstances take us there. Consequences resulting from poor judgment and bad decisions we've made take us there — to the edge of hopelessness — and we want to give up. There but for the grace of God go I. God understands the place we are in, and our state of mind. He knows what is really in our heart and which way we will go. He knows what the end will be and why. He knows that suicidal ideation or gestures is influenced by demonic forces that convince us to self-destruct. He also knows how He will intervene on our behalf in order to save us.

THE GREAT DECEPTION

I once read that suicide is an act of selfishness and a means of getting attention. The article stated that if a person were serious about committing suicide, they would go ahead and do it rather than make an announcement. When I thought about this, I concluded that there are other ways of getting attention that are far more positive. People don't just decide to kill themselves to be the talk of the day. There has to be more to this than a mere act of selfishness. There has to be a process that begins with a serious cry for help.

Personally, I didn't feel that I was being selfish when I tried to kill myself. I needed help. I wanted to be rescued from my self and my situation. People who commit suicide, or come close, have been crying out unnoticed for a long time. They needed someone to have a little compassion for their situation, but no compassion was offered. They needed someone to throw out the lifeline of hope, but no hope was found. They needed someone to be real with them, but what they received was deception. People who committed suicide as the way of escape were deceived to believe that there was no chance of them getting through their situation. They were robbed of all hope and convinced that they would never recover from their mistakes. They were deceived to believe that their life was worthless, and God had no purpose for them.

Suicide is directly influenced by a demonic spirit. God doesn't tell anyone to kill themselves. He doesn't whisper in our ear that we are worthless, or that we are without purpose. He doesn't leave us without hope or without comfort. God doesn't convince us that we'd be better off dead than alive. Anyone who hears those word in the depths of their soul needs to know that God is not speaking. In no uncertain terms, that's the voice of the devil. He's trying to convince you that you are nothing to God; and that, beloved, is a lie straight from the pits of Hell. The great deceiver has spoken death into your situation. He lied to your spirit.

Every chance the devil gets, he bum-rushes our mind with lies. He tries to make us feel unloved, unwanted, unappreciated, misunderstood and alone. He tells us that no one cares about us. He tells us that our friends and family don't care. He tries to convince us that they're only thinking about the insurance money and their inheritance. He tries to make us believe that someone deserves to hurt as much as we hurt and that by killing ourselves, they too will feel the pain we feel. Depression creeps into our spirit, and anger fills our heart. The devil convinces us that the only way to express our anger and relieve the pain is to hurt those who hurt us by committing suicide.

Talk about selfishness! Satan is the only one that's selfish. He's a self-absorbed lying wonder. All he wants is God's glory, power and authority. (Put another way, he wants to be God.) He wants to have power over life and death, and he thinks he can get it by causing man to kill himself and lose his soul. Satan is a thief, and he only wants to steal our soul. That's the plan! In suicide, the soul is surrendered to the consuming powers of darkness. In suicide, there is no repentance, so the devil uses it to keep man from turning to the safe arms of Jesus Christ our redeemer. Without the reservoir of salvation, it's easy to give in to the deception. Be assured that Jesus is our safe haven. In Him, we have hope, and suicide is not a true option.

SHHHHH! NOT IN THE CHURCH

While suicide is not a true option, let the truth be told. Some Believers have fallen to the devil's deceptions, too. Depression has no respect of persons. Some of us have suffered grief and depression to the point of wanting to end our lives. Some Believers have stood at the *crossroad* of sanity and insanity, depression and despair. The difference is that most of us were so afraid of dying and going to Hell that we prayed and asked God to intervene.

There are Christians hurting, right now, in our own church, and no one seems to be paying attention. We've turned a death ear and have covered our eyes to the depth of low self-esteem and the signs of depression. We ignore the fact that our brothers and sisters in Christ are hurting so deeply that they want to give up their faith and die. Not only has the church ignored suicidal ideation amongst the members, some churches don't want to address the issue at all. The topic is taboo. Suicidal ideation or gestures are often treated like an incurable disease from which we should stay away!

I remember growing up hearing that if a Saint committed suicide, they weren't really saved. Some churches were so self-righteous in their fundamental beliefs and practices that Believers who considered committing suicide were reluctant to talk with anyone about what they were going through. They were fearful that they would be rejected, scorned, put out of the church or declared "demon possessed" if they shared their thoughts about suicide. Rather than deal with the root of the situation, many Believers suppressed their pain and lived very bitter lives; or they were solemn and depressed.

Secrets of sin and pain buried deep within the sanctity of the church walls were also buried deep within the soul of the Saint. Some have lost their sanity because of the secrets buried in the back of their mind. They tried to maintain an outward appearance of being saved and sanctified, while inwardly they were filled with pain and cried silently.

For many years, the church-at-large did not provide it's members with professional mental health counseling. Rather, the scars of domestic violence, emotional abuse, rape, molestation, incest, teen pregnancy and unwed motherhood were covered up by religious fanaticism. Some Believers hid their anguish and despair behind the guise of over-zealousness and super sanctification. The chastisement of God was taught more than the love of God that extends grace and mercy. Rather than confess the truth about their state of mind and condition of spiritual torment, many Believers suffered silently until they couldn't handle the pressure any longer, and suicide became an option.

Times have changed, and the church-at-large more readily addresses the issues previously mentioned. Christian counselors are available for all people in all denominations. However, not all Believers utilize these resources. Some of us still suffer silently and continue to hide the emptiness in our heart and tormented spirit behind the facade of "working for Jesus." We stay so busy doing something in the name of Jesus that we tend to neglect our home, our family, our health, our appearance and our inner-self. We don't deal with the confusion in our mind, the heaviness of our emotions, the abuse and neglect we may suffer at home, or our unrepentant sins. To save face, we pretend that everything is all right, and we continue to live with pain. We'd rather breakdown internally than say we're hurting and need help.

We tend to hide behind the scripture, *"let the weakling say I am strong"* *(Joel 3:10)*, and we don't confront the true condition that makes us weak. All the while, we don't realize how our own denial makes us more vulnerable to Satan's deceptions. We are deceived to believe that the joy of the Lord, which is our strength, is not obtainable. Therefore, we stay weak in our spirit and in our mind. If the devil can get into our mind, he can get to our spirit. Our mind is where he plants the seed of self-destruction with the goal of destroying our soul. Clearly, the great deceiver is on the prowl seeking whom he can devour. Don't allow him to plant the seed of self-destruction in you.

We need to understand that the very elect of God can be deceived to believe that we don't deserve to live, or that the pain of life is too much for any one person to bear. When a Believer commits suicide, the devil has tricked them into believing that the Lord cannot keep them and bring them through the hardships of life. The cliche "Jesus Saves" is more than a declaration of salvation. It is a plea to the depressed, the down-trodden, the lonely, the broken-hearted and the weak-minded to cling to the horn of salvation. If the Believer, who is ready to let go of God to embrace death, can grab hold on to the mercies of God through the solid rock foundation of Jesus Christ, they will be saved — literally. Their life will be preserved by the saving grace of Jesus Christ.

JESUS SAVES

We have a Savior, an advocate, who feels what we feel. Jesus understands our loneliness. He knows about our depression and despondence. He knows all about rejection, denial and betrayal. He understands the complexities of every decision we make, and the results that follow. When we put our lives into the hands of the Savior, He will save us. He chose to lay down His life so that we could live. *"For God so loved the world that He gave His only begotten son that whosoever believeth in him should not perish, but have everlasting life. For God sent not his Son into the world to condemn the world; but that the world through him might be saved"* (John 3:16-17). No other self-sacrifice is acceptable.

Man cannot redeem himself through suicide. We are redeemed through the death, burial and resurrection of Jesus Christ. The Son chose to die. It was His sole reason for living. When the fullness of time had come, and Jesus was betrayed by Judas, He still had to choose whether or not to redeem man. As Jesus prepared Himself to be crucified, He knew that He could stop the process at anytime. He could have spoken to the waters and caused them to rise up and destroy the earth—as He did with the great flood. He could have turned the world inside out with just one breath, or remove His breath from the face of the earth and all life would have ceased. Instead, He called upon the Father to strengthen Him in His final hours.

To save man, Jesus girded up His loins and submitted to the Father's will. *"And He took with Him Peter and the two sons of Zebedee, and began to be sorrowful and very heavy. Then saith He unto them, My soul is exceeding sorrowful, even unto death: tarry ye here, and watch with me. And He went a little farther, and fell on His face, and prayed, saying, O my Father, if it be possible, let this cup pass from me: nevertheless not as I will, but as thou wilt"* (Matt. 26:37-39).

Surely the Lord had to consider whether or not man's soul was worth dying for. When Jesus observed His disciples Peter, James and John sleeping on the wayside as He labored in prayer before the Father, Jesus saw the frailty of mankind. He saw the innocence of His own creation, and man's vulnerability to Satan's deceptions. He was reminded of the fellowship with His beloved creation in the garden of Eden, and His betrayal by His own creation in the garden of Gethsemane. The love of God for us is so great that in spite of our rejection and betrayal, He willingly chose to reconcile us back to Himself. Not only did He declare to Satan that He is God, and the power of life and death is in His own hands, He also declared that man is worth saving. (We have value to God.)

PRAYER CHANGES THINGS

Change begins with prayer. Pray until something happens. Pray until you feel the change in your spirit. Pray until you feel the change in your heart. Pray until you turn. When Jesus prayed, the direction of the world turned. He prayed for the disciples who were chosen by the Father to believe in the Son. Through them, the world would come to know the Son. Through their witness, many others would believe on the Father and turn to Jesus for salvation. *"I have manifested thy name unto the men which thou gavest me out of the world: thine they were, and thou gavest them me, and they have kept thy word...I pray for them: I pray not for the world, but for them which thou hast given me; for they are thine. And all mine are thine, and thine are mine; and I am glorified in them"* (John 17:6, 9-10).

51

When Jesus prayed, He prayed for all who heard the Word of God and believed on Him without having first seen Him. Thereby, we were saved by grace according to our faith. Jesus prayed for our oneness in the Father through our oneness in the Son. *"Neither pray I for these alone, but for them also which shall believe on me through their word: that they all may be one; as thou, Father, art in me, and I in thee, that they also may be one in us: that the world may believe that thou hast sent me. And the glory which thou gavest me I have given them; that they may be one, even as we are one"* (John 17:20-23).

The same way that Jesus turned to the Father in prayer on behalf of His disciples and those who would believe in Him, we must do likewise for one another. We are obligated to stand watch for each other (as well as pray) during those times when suffering, loneliness, disparity, rejection and betrayal are upon the brethren. The Lord is depending on us to bear the infirmities of the weak and lead each other to the foot of the cross. We are commissioned to bring hope to the hopeless, comfort to the comfortless, and direction to the lost. The oneness of our prayers can touch the heart of God and cause Him to turn the situation around. The oneness of our prayers can make a difference in the lives of others and cause them to turn and make a change.

In my own distress and self-destructive behavior, somebody prayed for me. When I couldn't, wouldn't and didn't pray for myself, someone petitioned the Lord on my behalf. Someone prayed for me, even though they didn't know me personally or what I was going through. The ancestors prayed for me in the cotton fields when they prayed for deliverance from slavery. My family prayed for me down through the generations before I was even a thought in my parent's mind. My parents prayed for me from the moment they knew I was growing in my mother's womb. The Believers prayed for me when they asked God to bless my family. Someone in a little white church across town prayed for me when they said, "Lord save the unsaved." Jesus' prayer in the garden of Gethsemane was extended to me on the day of my salvation when I chose to accept Him as my Lord and Savior. (The prayers of intercession moved the hand of God on my behalf and kept me from slitting my wrists.)

I've been to the edge of hopelessness and sought to end my life more times than I can count. But prayer changed my heart. There was a time when I drowned my sorrows in shots of Rum (151 proof) and Southern Comfort chasers. I smoked more Black Gold and Cuban marijuana than I care to remember. I succumbed to sexual abuse and exploitation to the point that my emotions were numbed. I was drawn to death. I longed for it; hungered for it. I know what it is to be in a state of mind when emotional turmoil binds the ability to think rationally. My weeping endured through the night and lasted for days, weeks, months and years before the slightest sign of joy burst through the morning fog. I was at the *crossroads* of life and death (a critical turning point), and then I prayed. I turned to Jesus, and the Lord saved me. (Hallelujah!)

The words of David come to mind when I think about how my soul was gripped by despair, and the Lord heard my cry for help. He lifted my soul and saved me from death. *"The sorrows of death compassed me, and the pains of Hell gat hold upon me: I found trouble and sorrow. Then I called upon the name of the Lord: 'O Lord, I beseech thee, deliver my soul!' Gracious is the Lord, and righteous, yea, our God is merciful. The Lord preserveth the simple; I was brought low, and He helped me. Return unto your rest, O my soul, for the Lord has dealt bountifully with thee. For thou hast delivered my soul from death, mine eyes from tears, and my feet from falling"* (Psalm 116:3-8).

When you're at the *crossroads* (your turning point), and you don't know which way to go, pray. Prayer changes how we view our situation, and it opens our heart to options that we just don't see when we're angry or depressed. Because Christ abides in us and we in Him, we can call upon His name, and He will answer. This is our blessed assurance; the Lord is with us (always) in every situation. When we pray sincerely, He will change the direction of our lives. Then we will come to understand that everything we've ever been through and lived through was because the Lord brought us through. Every time He delivered us, He imbedded in our spirit a memory and a testimony for *the making of you*.

TURN

Every *crossroad* presents an opportunity to turn to Jesus. When we turn to Jesus, our path is made straight, and our direction is clear. Regardless of what we encountered during the journey; regardless of the obstacles that got in our way or the deceptions that caused us to err, we can still turn to Jesus. Jesus is right there waiting to help us. No matter how great the storm, how hard the wind may blow, how heavy the rain falls, how painful the hailstones, Jesus will protect us. When conditions impede our vision, and we can't see what lies ahead, we know that at the end of the road, our Savior is waiting with open arms and refreshments for our spirit. All we have to do is turn to Him. He's standing at the *crossroads* of life and death ready to lead us down the road of victory.

CHOSEN TO TURN

If you tried to commit suicide, or just thought about it, and you changed their mind, you are a living testimony. God chose you to be an example of His delivering power, and a witness to what He can do in you and through you. You were chosen to give the testimony of God's transforming power by the renewal of your mind. *"...Be ye transformed by the renewing of your mind, that ye may prove what is that good, and acceptable, and perfect will of God"* *(Romans 12:2).* You were chosen to turn to Jesus and be saved. You were given the chance to repent and turn to a life of holiness. *"Repent ye therefore and be converted that your sins may be blotted out, when the time of refreshing shall come from the presence of the Lord..."* *(Romans 8: 10, 11).* Only God can change our heart, transform our mind and restore His good, acceptable and perfect *will* in our lives. We were chosen for such a time as this to tell every nation that God changed our heart and restored our desire for life in those times when we wanted to die.

A CHANGED HEART

"Keep thy heart with all diligence; for out of it are the issues of life" (Proverbs 4:23). A heart that accepts Christ, accepts life. A heart that rejects Christ rejects God's love. To reject God's love is to die in our spirit.

In order to turn, God has to change our heart. We have to believe in the depths of our heart that God loves us individually and personally and so deeply that He sacrificed His own son, Jesus Christ, for our soul salvation. We have to believe that not only did God sacrifice His only begotten Son, the Son willfully gave His life for our redemption. We have to believe that a life in Christ is one hundred percent better than a life without Him.

Sure, we can rationalize, intellectualize and analyze how God can love His creation so much that He initiated a plan of salvation that cannot be duplicated; and we can conceptualize the logic of the need for redemption, but it's with our heart that we respond to the suffering of Christ on the cross and are compelled to conversion. Our heart responds to God's love, and reciprocates His love through our faith, obedience, kindness, compassion and service. Because we have a changed heart, we can become the vessels God uses to infuse life into a dying world, heal the broken-hearted, bring sanity and order to the confused mind, peace to the tormented soul and understanding to the bewildered spirit.

TURN AWAY FROM GUILT AND SHAME

A changed heart accepts change; a changed heart turns away from sin and accepts forgiveness. Regardless of the nature of our sin, God forgives and cleanses us thoroughly. Whether they were/are sins of omission or commission, we can be cleansed. David declared, *"...cleanse thou me from secret faults. Keep back thy servant also from presumptuous sins..." (Psalm 19: 12-13).*

Once we've turned from sin, we need to leave the stain of sin behind. What is the stain of sin? Guilt and shame! When God forgives us of our sins, we are cleansed and made whole. There is no residue—there is no stain. *"... though your sins be as scarlet, they shall be as white as snow; though they be red like crimson, they shall be as wool" (Isaiah 1:18).*

We are washed by the blood of the lamb, and our sins are cast into the sea of forgetfulness. Like the children of Israel to whom God showed mercy and cast their sins into the sea, we can say,

"Who is a God like unto thee, that pardoneth iniquity, and passeth by the transgressions of the remnant of His heritage? He retaineth not his anger forever, because He delighteth in mercy. He will turn again, He will have compassion upon us; He will subdue our iniquities, and thou wilt cast all their sins into the depths of the sea" (Micah 7:18-19).

We have a new covenant with Jesus Christ, and our sins are remembered no more. *"This is the covenant that I will make with them after those days, saith the Lord, I will put my law into their hearts, and in their minds will I write them; and their sins and iniquities will I remember no more"*(Hebrews 10:16-17).

We are no longer under condemnation. *"There is therefore now no condemnation to them which are in Christ Jesus, who walk not after the flesh, but after the Spirit. For the law of the Spirit of life in Christ Jesus hath made me free from the law of sin and death"* (Rom. 8:1-2).

God has forgiven us, cast our sins into the sea and remembers them no more. He grants us everlasting mercy and compassion. Why then do we continue to walk with the heaviness of past sin weighing on our conscious? Christ has freed us through salvation. There is no place for the guilt and shame of past sins for which we have been forgiven. Paul admonishes us; as he did the Galatians, to: *"Stand fast therefore in the liberty wherewith Christ hath made us free, and be not entangled again with the yoke of bondage"* *(Galatians 5:1).* When we were freed from the bondage of sin, we were also freed from the yoke of guilt and shame. Because we are free, we have the peace of God through our Lord and Savior Jesus Christ.

TURN TO A PLACE OF REST

The Lord has touched our lives and turned our hopelessness into hopefulness. He has forgiven us and cleansed us of our sin. He has removed the scarlet stain of sin (the yoke of guilt and shame) and sanctified us unto Himself. He has created a new heart within us and renewed us with His Holy Spirit. For the spirit of heaviness, He has given us a garment of praise.

The Lord has delivered us from the hands of the thief that comes to steal our soul, and we are free to live life more abundantly in Christ Jesus. Now is the time to enter into a place of rest. Our weary soul has longed for this place of rest, and the Lord is willing to accommodate us.

Let us rejoice in knowing that at every turning point, God is with us, and He brings us to a place of rest. He leads us to the still waters that refresh our soul and quickens our spirit. The table is spread before our enemy (the devourer of souls), and we can feast on the goodness of the Lord in peace. The Lord gives us sweet peace when we lay our burdens and heaviness on Him. He will carry them all. He is our resting place; He is our peace.

Receive these words in your spirit and be comforted. *"Come unto me, all ye that labor and are heavy laden, and I will give you rest. Take my yoke upon you, and learn of me; for I am meek and lowly in heart: and ye shall find rest unto your souls. For my yoke is easy, and my burden is light"* (Matthew 11:28-30).

TURN YOUR TRAGEDY INTO A TESTIMONY

I wanted to commit suicide as both a sinner and a Saint, and God's love saved me. He wouldn't allow me to end my own life. When I think about the many *crossroads* and turning points I faced, I know that God was with me. I wouldn't be here today if the Lord were not walking with me and carrying me and upholding me with His spirit. Every time I made a bad decision and exercised poor judgment, God turned the situation around for my good. Every time I entered into a relationship that had "Dead End" posted on the wall, and I felt as though my heart couldn't take the pain, God comforted me and awakened me from an emotional coma. Every time I allowed myself to get into a situation that I had no business being in, God rescued me. Every time my spirit crossed the spirit of darkness, God sent a host of angels to build a barricade around me with their wings; He sent the warrior angels with flaming swords to fight the demons that wanted to steal my soul. The Lord embraced me with mercy, loved me with chastisement, and upheld me with grace.

Today, I am a witness that God loved me through sorrow and despair. He saved me from sin and self-destruction. He turned my tragedy into a testimony. I know He will do the same for you when you turn to Jesus. (To God be the glory. Hallelujah!)

Reflections

1) Prayer changes things. Pray until your change comes.

2) Write down a scripture that gives you encouragement and put it on your bedroom mirror, or closet door. Meditate on it daily.

3) Suicide is not an option! Jesus loves you too much to leave you comfortless and without hope. Turn to Jesus. He will help you.

4) If you have suicidal thoughts, seek professional help and godly counsel from a pastor, minister or Christian counselor.

This is my prayer

"But thou, O Lord art a shield for me; my glory, and the lifter up of mine head" (Psalm 3:3).

You, Lord, are my strength and my Redeemer. You are my fortress and a very present help in the time of trouble. When I call upon your name, you answer. In the midst of turmoil, you send peace. You comfort my soul. Your spirit brings direction to my indecision. You infuse clarity where there is confusion. When I want to give up, you embrace me with love and gird my loins with holiness.

I put my trust in you, O Lord. For I know that you are my deliverer. Help me to turn away from self-destructive thoughts and behavior and turn to the light of my salvation. Renew your spirit in me. Renew my mind and transform my life from helplessness to hopefulness. Restore your joy in me and lead me to the rock that is higher than I. Keep me on the path of righteousness.

Thank you, Lord, for turning my life around. I exalt you, God of my salvation, for your love and mercy endures forever. Amen.

THREE

THEY SAID
(Nay-Sayers)

"For it was not an enemy that reproached me; then I could have borne it: neither was it he that hated me that did magnify himself against me; then I would have hid myself from him: But it was thou, a man mine equal, my guide, and mine acquaintance. We took sweet counsel together, and walked unto the house of God in company" (Psalms 55:12-14).

"Let us not therefore judge one another any more: but judge this rather, that no man put a stumbling block or an occasion to fall in his brother's way" (Romans 14:13).

"Out of the same mouth proceedeth blessing and cursing. My brethren, these things ought not so to be" (James 3:10).

YOU TALK'N 'BOUT ME?

They were talking about me, and I heard them. They said I wouldn't last a month. They said I wasn't even saved. They said (a Believer said) that I wouldn't stay saved (if I was saved), for more than one month. How could that be? How could They say that about me? Just one month? This Great joy that I have; this refreshing bliss; this release from sin would only last a month? They said a lot of things about me. Many hurtful things that cut to the very core of my soul. They're still talking about me! They'll probably be talking about me tomorrow, too!

THE DAY OF SALVATION

The day I accepted salvation, my heart was convicted, and my soul converted. I made a conscious decision to follow Christ. I wanted to be saved. I was ready for a change, and a change had come. When my stony heart became flesh, I gave up the ways of my past and gave in to the ways of Christ. It was a decision I gladly made, and a new life I was eager to receive. In that precious and glorious moment of salvation, I didn't think about whether or not I would go back into a life of sin. I didn't think about whether or not I would put a cigarette in my mouth or get drunk or indulge in sexual exploits. Neither did I think about what my friends would say. I was running for my life, literally, and I wanted God to save me.

When I stepped down into the baptismal pool, I had already surrendered my heart to the Lord. My heart was converted long before my foot even touched the water. No one coerced me into being baptized. I did it of my own free *will*. When the baptismal water wrapped around my body, and I was fully submerged, the anointing of the Holy Spirit wrapped around my soul. My sins were buried with Christ. When I emerged, I came up rejoicing in the newness of a resurrected life. The evidence of the Holy Spirit was upon me as my lips began to stammer with another tongue. Praises filled the room, and I heard myself crying out, "Thank you Jesus. Thank you Jesus." I leaped for joy right there in the pool. God saved me! I wasn't concerned about who was standing at the side of the pool watching, nor did I focus on the songs the witnesses were singing. My focus was on Jesus. He and I had a personal moment together as He washed my soul and sanctified me unto Himself. Nothing else was important to me at the time.

After I dressed, I was escorted into the "tarry room" where the deacons and missionaries prayed with me. I remember calling on the name of the Lord Jesus and giving Him thanks for saving my soul. I was so grateful to God for saving me—that He didn't cut my life short while I was still in sin. Oh what a glorious day! When I surrendered to the Lord, I surrendered my all. There was no holding on to the past. (What for?) I was so grateful that when the deacon told me to get on my knees and see the cross and call Jesus, there was no hesitation and no resistance. My stubborn *will* was washed away. On my knees I went—praying, calling Jesus, spitting and slobbering while the Holy Spirit purged my soul of demonic influence. This was not a show. There was no pretense. There was no one to impress. God was dealing with me, purging me and delivering me.

The Believers in the prayer room didn't fully know why I was thanking God (other than a change had come.) They didn't know the details of my life. They didn't know what I had been through, where I had been, the things I had done, nor the things I had seen and heard. They didn't ask my life story before I could be baptized, or force me to give a full confession of what I had done. They weren't interested in whether or not I had a job, lived in a house or apartment, carried American Express or Visa, graduated from high school or went to college. They were concerned about my soul. They were there to help me to see

Jesus. They were there to pray with me and praise God with me and labor with me until the Lord fully endowed me with the precious gift of His Holy Spirit (with the full evidence of speaking in tongues as the Spirit of God gave utterance, not just stammering lips—bua, bua, bua, bua, bua).

In those days, there was no such thing as, "it didn't take" (like a hair perm that didn't take). There was no such thing as, "Say it like this; tidiupmybowtie, hecominhonda, hickamasya." No one whispered in your ear the words to say, and you weren't taught how to speak in tongues "the right way." When the spirit of the Lord filled a Believer, He confirmed the infilling with a genuine tongue that could not be duplicated with practice. The spirit gives witness to the spirit. Beloved, I tell you a truth. When God fills you with His spirit, you know it for yourself. You don't have to wonder or guess or wait for someone to say, "you got it."

You will hear yourself speaking in tongues. You will feel the Holy Spirit filling your soul. You "will" know! You won't have to come back tomorrow because "it didn't take," or you were just partially filled. What kind of God is God that He would only fill us with His spirit "a little bit" so that we have to come back and get the rest another day? (There is one initial infilling of the Holy Spirit and many refills for our spiritual renewal.) When the Lord fills us, it is a complete filling. There's no such thing as a partial infilling of the Holy Spirit. Either you're filled with the Holy Spirit, or you're not. Either you've spoken in tongues as the Spirit of God gives utterance (as evidence of the initial infilling of the Holy Spirit), or you didn't.

When God filled me with His Holy Spirit, I was full. There was no doubt and no question. I knew what the Lord had done in me. The Spirit of God spoke expressly in utterances of a language interpreted only by God Himself. God spoke to my heart, and a covenant between my Lord and I was declared in the heavens. The Lord took time to talk with me, personally, without the assistance of the on-lookers. I felt so relieved and so free that I began to dance a dance I had never danced before. (It wasn't straight up and down, or side to side with a rhythmic motion induced by the clapping of hands, a drum beat or an organ playing a "vamp.") I couldn't control my feet, and I couldn't control my tongue. I felt different. I felt fresh. My head felt lighter. I could feel the "Kool-Aid" smile stretching my cheek muscles as the tears streaming down my face washed my soul. My God and I were having a private conversation, and the angels hosted a celestial celebration for my soul salvation.

I was overwhelmed with gratitude because God accepted me as His child. Yes, God accepted me—all that I was and all that I wasn't, God accepted me on that glorious day of my salvation.

A SHOCK TO MY SYSTEM

I was saved, sanctified (set aside by God for His purpose) and filled with the Holy Spirit. I was made whole by a single touch of the Master's hand. Then it happened. I don't believe it was more than two weeks later, after a soul-stirring Holy Ghost filled prayer service, the Believers were going home when I overheard a conversation in the stairwell. "It won't last. I give her a month. She won't stay saved." There they were, a preacher and a deacon, talking about me. Who else could they have been talking about? I was the only new convert in the prayer service that night! How could they say that about me? What had I done to them to merit such a comment? Was the Holy Spirit so impotent that He couldn't keep me saved more than a month? I was devastated when I heard what they said. Even though I testified and shared some of what the Lord had saved me from, they really didn't know me. I believed God would keep me. Why couldn't they believe God for me?

What an injustice! I felt betrayed. As Psalm 55: 12-14 declares, "It *wasn't an enemy, or someone that hated me that reviled themselves against me..."* Were that the case, I could have handled it. I knew where my enemies stood. My enemies didn't keep their feelings of jealously, hatred, envy and malice hidden from my view. It was my brothers in Christ that spoke out against me; not an acquaintance. Someone with whom I was familiar and trusted for guidance. Someone who prayed with me and gained my confidence and trust. Someone whom God declared my equal in Christ, a co-laborer in the kingdom, joint heirs to the throne. We fellowshipped and sang the songs of Zion together. Didn't that count for anything?

I was on top of the world because God saved me. I drank of the new wine and was drunk in the spirit for days. Nothing could touch me. Then crash, bang, smash'em up! My euphoric state of mind was under attack. My heart was crushed, as was my spirit. What a shock to my system! Someone forgot to tell me that the devil attacks us after we accept salvation because he's trying to keep us from totally committing ourselves to the service of the Lord.

I was hurt (to say the least) and discouraged. Doubt set in, and I questioned my own salvation. I believed God saved me, yet after hearing those words, I wondered if I was truly saved. I doubted my commitment to God and wondered if I would turn back to the sins of the past. As a new-born babe; a new convert, I was anxious and zealous, but I didn't know God's keeping power. I didn't know if I would be strong enough to resist temptation. God delivered me from my circumstances, but I wondered if I could stay delivered. Let's face it, when the crisis ends, we sometimes forget the Savior who delivered us, and the promises we made to God if He would deliver us. Where was my faith? Did I have enough faith to stand? Could I stand? I wasn't sure anymore.

DEFENSE MODE

In self-defense, I found myself feeling the need to prove the proverbial "they" that they were wrong about me. After all, who were "they" anyway? "They" had no right to decide my spiritual fate. "They" had no right to judge me. "They" didn't know my heart. "They" didn't pay my bills. "They" didn't take care of my home. "They" were just the people at church. I told myself that when I went home from service every Sunday, "they" weren't coming home with me. So what did "they" matter to me? (What a mess.)

I was on a new mission to become "Super Saved." I had to prove to everyone that I was really saved, sanctified and filled with the Holy Ghost. That was my only logical defense; to over do it. That's how I dealt with my feelings of inadequacy when I wasn't saved; I forced myself to excel beyond what was expected or required of me. Surely the same tactic would suffice now that I'm saved.

It was the story of my life; whatever it was "they" said about me, I had to prove them wrong. "They" said I wouldn't make it and that I would amount to nothing. So I excelled academically to prove that I was smart and could do anything I wanted to do. "They" said I wasn't good enough to be with the in-crowd. So I formed my own in-crowd. "They" said I would never date the handsome and popular guys in school. Well, I made it my business to acquaint myself with the very ones "they" said I wouldn't date. Whatever negative thing "they" said; whether "they" were friends, family, foe or society, I did just the opposite to prove them wrong. No one was going to put me in a box and determine who I was or what I could do. I was of the mind set that I couldn't allow anyone to define my abilities and capabilities, or label and stereotype me because of their own opinions or shortcomings. Hence, I erroneously compromised myself, my values and my virtue just to keep "them" from being right! (That was hard work!)

That same attitude quickly resurfaced when I heard what "they" said about me while standing in the church stairwell. I found myself relying on old tactics. Rather than wait on the Holy Spirit to move within me and mature me, I was determined to fight a spiritual battle I had no business trying to fight. Rather than rely on the Holy Spirit, I relied on my own intellect and natural abilities to battle the nay-sayers. I was spiritually immature trying to be someone and something that I really wasn't. The result, of course, was that I developed an attitude of self-righteousness. I had become a Pharisee — sanctimonious and ritualistic. My mind was clouded by the devil's deceptive devices that caused me to believe that I had "arrived." (I was only fooling myself.)

VULNERABLE BABES

When we are babes in Christ, we are extremely sensitive and vulnerable to criticism. We don't know the scriptures well. We don't understand the power of God within us. We don't know our spiritual potential, nor the tests, trials and persecution that awaits us. We don't know the suffering and tribulation that we will face for Christ's sake. Often, we're not even sure of what we believe, other than Jesus saved us from sin and changed our lives. We don't know all the nuances of salvation or what's going on in the spirit realm. Neither do we know the spiritual traps the devil sets in our path to cut us off before we begin to grow.

Our faith is not yet fully developed, and we have not established spiritual fortitude and stamina. We are learning the scriptures, but we are not yet rooted and grounded in the Word of God. Primarily, we are adapting to a new lifestyle that tells us to dress, look and act a "peculiar" way. We're excited, zealous, happy and willing Believers hungry for the Word and ready to receive. Our mind, heart and spirit are vast receptacles waiting to be filled. We are an open door for spiritual endowment. As such, we are potential recipients of God's anointing, as well as the influence of deceptive and counterfeit spirits. Even though we may feel that something is not right, we may not have the knowledge, wisdom, experience or discernment to know the difference between the workings of the Holy Spirit and the deceptions of demonic influence. We are vulnerable to the devil's folly!

Like babes in the natural, our initial spiritual learning comes through our senses...particularly through sight and sound. With the portholes of vision and hearing open to receive, what we see and hear as new Believers becomes the foundation of our faith and influences the direction of our spiritual growth and maturity. When we are constantly exposed to criticism, negativism, doubt, fear and discouragement, our spiritual growth can be hindered. We can lose confidence in ourselves and in our salvation, and we can waiver in our belief. Sometimes, our own behavior reflects the doubtful and negative attitudes we see portrayed by people we hold in high regard. (Spirits are transferable.)

The transference of negative attitudes gets played out in our worship and service in the church. Inadvertently, we become the "they" that are talking about other Believers, new comers and people in the church that we don't like. We can develop an attitude of piety and boast about what we would do if we were the president of the New York Club, the Missionary Department or the Pastor's Aide. Nothing is ever good enough, or to our liking. We always have something to say about something or someone, and our name can be heard in every conversation (though not always in a positive way). We become back-biters, gossipers and arrogant in all of our ways.

If, on the other hand, we are nourished with truth, positive encouragement, and the righteousness of God's Word, our soul will prosper. Our faith is strengthened by hearing the Word of God. *"So then faith cometh by hearing, and hearing by the word of God"* (Romans 10:17). If what we hear is not the Word of God, but corrupt communication, our spirit will be subjected to corruption rather than increased faith.

Words can either build or cripple us when we are new to salvation. Words can either erect a barrier to keep the influence of the devil out, or they can create a stumbling block that affects the direction of our Christian journey. So the next time the Pastor is preaching, and you're making negative comments about every word that comes out of his or her mouth, ask yourself the question, "Am I guilty of creating stumbling blocks for the people sitting around me because of something I said?" Someone is as vulnerable as you once were, and your words may make a difference in their spiritual growth and development.

WORDS THAT BUILD UP OR TEAR DOWN

Our mouth is a vicious weapon that can destroy any good thing with just one word— "But." The interjection of "but" infers doubt. "She was baptized last week, but..." "I believe she's saved, but..." "I feel the power of God in me, but..." "There's something the Lord has for me to do, but..." The word "but" can be a road block to a Believer's success. "But" destroys. Most often when we use the word "but," we can be sure that the next words will be something negative or derogatory that infers doubt. The use of the word "but" when describing a person's character or actions tends to be an unconscious (though sometimes quite deliberate) attempt to assassinate that person's character. The imposed "but" allows for speculation, concern and distrust.

We speak good about a person out of one side of our mouth, and bad out of the other side. We spew both blessings and curses at the same time. James clearly let's us know that the tongue is an untamable, poisonous and vicious weapon that is capable of disseminating both blessings and curses. *"But the tongue can no man tame; it is an unruly evil, full of deadly poison....Out of the same mouth proceedeth blessings and cursing..."* (James 3:8, 10).

Why do we bless one another when we're talking face to face, or in the presence of the general congregation, and then curse one another in private conversations with other Believers? Why do we say one thing to a person's face and something else behind their back? Do we really believe that we're building ourselves up when we highlight someone else's character flaws? Think again! The more we talk about each other with negativism, the more we reveal our own character flaws; the more we mirror the true motives of our own heart. Corrupt communication reflects a corrupt heart.

When we talk about each other, we are passing judgment, and our wicked tongues disperse seeds of destruction. Have we forgotten that we are judged by the same measure of judgment we impose on others? *"Judge not, that ye be not judged. For with what judgment ye judge, ye shall be judged: and with what measure ye mete, it shall be measured to you again"* (Matthew 7:1-2). Paul asked the question, *"But why dost thou judge thy brother? Or why dost thou set at naught thy brother? For we shall all stand before the judgment seat of Christ"* (Romans 14:10). (Just a reminder, we all will face judgment when we stand before the White Throne of Judgment.)

Personal judgment in the Body of Christ causes dispersion, disharmony, disunity, distrust, discord, disassociation, dislike, disgust and dishonor. All of which leads to broken fellowship among the brethren. When discord enters the Church Body, confusion and division rules the house, and the ministry becomes ineffective. Our judgment becomes a stumbling block for someone else. Paul, admonished the Believers, *"… Let us not therefore judge one another any more: but judge this rather, that no man put a stumbling block or an occasion to fall in his brother's way"* (Romans 14:13).

Our words will either build up or tear down. Even what we say in jest can either build or destroy. People take what we say seriously more times than not, especially if we're in a position of leadership and authority. Therefore, it behooves us to stop talking about one another! The person doing the talking stands in judgment of whomever it is they're talking about. The person being talked about becomes a marked target for ridicule, rejection and defamation of character, and they may not recover from the injury. The persons engaged in the conversation somehow get coerced into back-biting and gossiping. All parties involved are given an occasion to stumble and fall because of something "they" said. Let's not be guilty of being a stumbling block and bringing destruction when we can be builders of the Faith instead. (God forgive us!)

GO WITH WHAT YOU KNOW

In retrospect, only the grace of God kept me from falling when I heard the words, "it won't last." I knew in my heart that I was sincere about my salvation. I leaned on the fact that God knew all about me and had already preordained my destiny. Regardless of what anyone had to say, or thought about me, my ability to stay saved or return to the things of the world were already known to the Father. The way of escape and deliverance were already prepared. God knew what He delivered me from, and He knew whether or not I would stay delivered. In spite of what "they" said, and in spite of my defensiveness, I held fast to the knowledge that Jesus loved me and could keep me from falling — if I wanted to be kept. (I decided that I wanted to be kept.)

Certainly I was discouraged and had become hard-hearted for a season, but I promised the Lord that I would serve Him until I die. To work out my own salvation, I had to hold on to what I knew. I knew that I was saved. I knew that the Lord loved me. I knew that I didn't want to fall from grace. I knew that God was able to keep me saved. I knew that I had an advocate in the Son. Jesus would be my strength. Jesus would help me like He did so many times before. I knew the Word of God would strengthen me and empower me to hold on just a little while longer. I knew that the Holy Spirit would lead and guide me into all truth and righteousness. I knew that if I gave in to what "they" said, I would lose my salvation and die. (I wanted to live!) The words of the song "I Shall Not Be Moved" penetrated my spirit, and I became more determined to hold fast to my salvation. Like the tree planted by the rivers of water, I was determined not to be moved (Psalm 1:3).

God, in His infinite mercy, assured me that I belonged to Him. His hand was upon me, and I was sealed by His Holy Spirit. In time, the Lord began to temper me and replace my arrogance with meekness, and self-righteousness with humility. Going through wasn't easy, but God helped me. I didn't always want to be meek and humble, but the Lord had to work meekness and humility into my character. It was painful at times, and I cried most of the time. There were times when I wanted to give up; and there were times when I did give up (which we'll talk about later), and God restored me. Now I know for myself that God is a keeper for those who want to be kept because He kept me.

When you hear the Believers talking about you, and you feel discouraged, hold fast to what you know. You know that Jesus loves you. You know that you love Him and desire to serve the Lord with all your heart, body, soul, mind and spirit. You know that you are special to the Father, and that He has already planned your destiny. You know that what God blesses is blessed; and what God curses is cursed. Since God has blessed you, no man can curse you. You know that the Holy Spirit is a keeping power and will keep you from falling if you want to be kept. You know that no matter what the people say, you are going on in the name of the Lord.

When you observe that the same mouth which blesses you is also spewing out curses against you, *"The words of his mouth were smoother than butter, but war was in his heart: his words were softer than oil, yet were they drawn swords" (Psalm 55:21),* take comfort in knowing that you can, *"Cast thy burden upon the Lord, and he shall sustain thee: he shall never suffer the righteous to be moved" (Psalm 55:22).* When you feel that your character is under attack, and you are discouraged by the negativism and doubt in what "they" said, remember that you belong to God. You are established by the One who sacrificed His life for your salvation, Jesus. You are bought with a price and adopted into the royal family as joint heirs to the throne. Your life in Christ is predestined and purposed. *"In whom also we have obtained an inheritance, being predestined according to the purpose of Him who worketh all things after the counsel of His own will" (Ephesians 1:11).*

The same God whom you trusted to deliver you from sin unto salvation by the hearing of the Word, *"In whom ye also trusted, after that ye heard the word of truth, the gospel of your salvation: in whom also after that ye believed, ye were sealed with that Holy Spirit of promise" (Ephesians 1:3),* is the same God that will deliver you and strengthen you in the presence of the nay-sayers. Remember that you are anointed and sealed by the Holy Spirit. *"Now He which stablisheth us with you in Christ, and hath anointed us, is God; who hath also sealed us, and given the earnest of the spirit in our hearts" (2 Corinthians 1:21-22).* You are who and what God says you are regardless of what "they" said.

REALITY CHECK

Just in case no one ever told you, let me be the first. As long as you have a desire to serve God and stay in fellowship with Christ, you will encounter the destructive power of the tongue. It is the work of the devil. His objective is to separate us from God, and his strategy is to sow seeds of discord into the Body of Christ. He tries to destroy the oneness of God amongst the Believers in order to keep us from achieving unity. When the people of God are unified, the power of God comes through like a mighty rushing wind. If the devil can keep us murmuring about each other and sowing seeds of discord and suspicion, he can keep us from being a powerful force of healing and deliverance in the kingdom of God.

A small muscle in our mouth that was created to bless God can easily be defiled and used as a silver-tipped blade in the devil's artillery. He used this weapon to deceive Eve in the garden of Eden, and he used it when Adam blamed Eve for his own disobedience. He used it to convict and crucify our Lord Jesus, and he used it to bring dissension among the Believers of the first church. He uses it today to destroy that good and perfect *will* of God in our lives, and he uses it to break the bonds of fellowship between God and His people.

We are the beloved of God, and we are blessed by God. If God is for us, who can be against us? What weapon formed against us will ever prosper? The weapon of the tongue may cut us up pretty badly and leave us wounded, but we don't have to die. We can recover from what "they" said...with the help of the Lord. We are made strong through adversity. If we can endure what "they" said, we will gain strength and fortitude to endure the greater adversities that are sure to come.

Reflections

1. What do you do when you know another Christian is talking about you? How do you respond when someone comes to you and talks about another Believer?

2. Stop and pray. We don't have to be used by the devil to sow seeds of dissention into the Body of Christ. When we feel the urge to talk about the Believers, pass judgment and discredit them in order to build ourselves up; or when we feel victimized by the ones who are talking about us, stop and pray. We don't have to become defensive and resort to old tactics. Neither do we have to reciprocate with malicious words that destroy. God will control our tongue (and the tongue of others) when we pray.

3. Someone, somewhere will have something to say about you. That's just the adversary doing what he does. We don't have to let what "they" said paralyze us or cause us to fall away from the Faith. Don't stay stuck in what

"they" said. Gird up your loins, let it go and move on!

This is my Prayer

"Father, forgive them for they know not what they do" (Luke 23:34).

Lord, forgive me for my evil thoughts towards those who have spewed out corrupt communication concerning me. Please forgive me for imposing the same infraction upon others. Forgive my judgments. Cleanse my heart, my mind and my spirit.

Father, look upon those that are young in the Lord and give them strength to endure. Fortify them through your Word, and deliver them from wicked communication. Put a song of praise on their lips and a melody in their heart that will encourage them during the rough times.

Lord, Cause our lips to bless you and your people. Help us to exalt one another above ourselves, and to build each other up rather than to tear each other down. In Jesus' name. Amen.

FOUR

WHEN THE TEMPTER COMES
(Temptation)

*"Wherefore let him that thinketh he
standeth take heed lest he fall. There
hath no temptation taken you but such
as is common to man: but God is
faithful, who will not suffer you to be
tempted above that ye are able: but will
with the temptation also make a way to
escape, that ye may be able to bear it"* (I
Corinthians 10:12-13).

*"As for God, his way is perfect: the
word of the Lord is tried: he is a buckler
to all those that trust in him. For who is
God save the Lord? Or who is a rock
save our God? It is God that girdeth me
with strength, and maketh my way
perfect"* (Psalm 18:30-32).

89

Reverend Michele Taylor

EVERYTHING'S JUST FINE

You're rooted and grounded in the Word of God and have a solid foundation. You drank the milk of the Word and are now feasting on the meat of the Word. You've gained substance, wisdom and knowledge. The things that once bothered you and shook your faith as a young Christian don't affect you the same way as they did in your earlier years of salvation. You stopped trying to convince the nay-sayers that you're saved, sanctified and filled with the Holy Ghost. What "they said" no longer grips your spirit and offends you. You've grown up some, and are standing tall in Christ!

You've adjusted to church life, and you've learned that no one is perfect, save Jesus Christ our redeemer. You understand that the imperfections of the Believers, including your own, are character flaws common to all mankind. You're maturing in the Lord and are growing in grace daily. Your attitude has also changed. You're tempered, and the fruit of the spirit is manifested in your life. You now know that man's words are subjective and filled with self-rewarding motives, while God's Word is objective and true. You're not offended when someone tells you they don't believe in Jesus because you know He's real just the same. You've memorized your response to the non-believer. *"For what if some did not believe? Shall their unbelief make the faith of God without effect? God forbid: yea, let God be true, but every man a liar; as it is written, that thou mightest be justified in thy sayings, and mightest overcome when thou are judged"* (Romans 3:3-4).

Finally, you can stand as a defender of the faith. You have experience! You participate in all the major church activities and services. You are faithful, dependable, reliable and trustworthy. Everything's just fine. There's nothing to complain about, and you're running on in the name of the Lord. New heights abound every day.

FACE TO FACE

Without warning, you come face to face with a moment of temptation that seemed to have come out of nowhere. There you are standing toe to toe, face to face, with temptation. As strong as your faith is, and your commitment to God's service, the very thing that you fled from when you first accepted Christ as your personal Savior is now staring you in the face. Just when you thought you had this thing down pat; your past was in the past and your Christian life is thriving—Oops, there it is! Temptation.

"Where did this come from?" You might ask. You stopped smoking, and suddenly after two years, you have an urge to put a cigarette in your mouth. You gave up drinking, but for some reason, you feel the desire to down a 40 (40 oz. bottle of beer). Your days of promiscuity are over, and you now have an intense desire to do-the-do. You bumped into an old flame, and your emotions got stirred up by memories of the passion between you. A forbidden love interest pulls on your heart-strings, or you just cannot resist scratching that Lotto ticket. Regardless of the nature of the temptation, for a moment, you are rocked — thrown off balance. You can't seem to get yourself together. You want "it" (whatever the "IT" is). You toil over getting it; "should I, or shouldn't I." Your mind plays tricks with you, and you find yourself drifting away into your deepest imaginations.

THE "WHAT IF'S"

The "What If's" infiltrate your thoughts like the head of a drill burrowing into the depths of an oil well. What if I take one puff? What if I drink that 40? What if I take home that old broken down typewriter that no one uses without asking my supervisor? What if I go clubbing and dance the night away? What if I stop by so-and-so's house for just a minute while his wife isn't home? What if I "do it" just this one time? What if I make that phone call to sister red-dress? What if I give in to my passions? Though the thought of these things may or may not be a direct or immediate crisis, giving in to our temptations can lead to major spiritual conflict. We are tempted every day of our lives to tamper with the little things we enjoyed in the past, or things that now peak our interest.

The What If's do come. That's a fact, a promise and a guarantee. We cannot escape the What If's from beckoning our door. We can, however, resist. Does the word "No" mean anything? Yes, it does. We can say No to every temptation that we encounter. We have the right to say No. Lives have been saved (literally) with the simple use of the word No. Saying No is a strong line of defense. It immediately sets in place a barrier. Saying No imposes an invisible stop sign that affords us time to stop, look and think before acting on the temptation. Saying No gives us time to reach into our soul and find our desire for righteousness.

Because our desire for righteousness is greater than our desire for pleasure, we will focus on pleasing God and not our flesh. The flesh does not have to rule! Though we often allow it to control us, the flesh can be controlled. The Holy

Spirit that abides in us helps us to exercise self-control. The same way the Holy Spirit helps us to control our tongue from spewing out obscenities and corrupt communication, it will help us to put our flesh under subjection. We can say "No" to temptation and walk away from its presence. The Holy Spirit will do that in us and for us.

The questions to ask yourself are, "What do I really want to do? Do I want to be caught in my sin, or do I want to overcome my weakness?" Whether or not we get caught and are brought to an open shame, God sees what we're doing, and we are "busted" in His sight. If we think within ourselves, "No body's watching." Think again; God is watching, and He knows. He will always catch us in our sin—when we give in to temptation. If we ask ourselves the soul-searching questions that evaluate where we are spiritually and where we want to be, we can answer ourselves honestly and make a decision. Whatever our decision; to sin or not to sin when we are faced with the smallest or greatest temptations, we have to be honest with ourselves and with God. We can't lie to God because He already knows the truth, so we're really just lying to ourselves. Telling ourselves the truth about how we feel and what's going on inside of us will help us to confront our temptations and say No.

TEMPTED

For the record, God does not tempt us. Temptation comes from the devil. His purpose, quite simply, is to cause us to sin. Sin separates us from God. Sin drives a wedge between us and our God. It puts a strain on our relationship with the Father. Though the Lord still loves us when we fall, giving in to temptation causes us to fall away from what we know and believe to be the truth of God's Word. Giving in to temptation can cause us to waver in our faith, or turn completely away from the Faith and return to our former ways. Sin leads to death—spiritual death, *"for the wages of sin is death…" (Romans 6:23)*. We are tempted because the devil wants to kill us spiritually. He will also try to kill us physically so that we won't have a chance to repent and be restored spiritually.

LIES, LIES AND MORE LIES

Temptation is a lie that appeals to man's innate desire to be like God—as man is created in the image of God. Temptation is a lie orchestrated by the father of the lie. The devil is a liar, and the father of all lies! That's who he is and what he does. He's been telling lies from the very beginning, and he'll continue to tell lies until the end of his time. He lies to us every day, and in every way that appeals to man.

The devil lied to the heavenly host of angels and convinced one third of them to believe that he should be God. Consequently, he and his followers were kicked out of heaven. Then he lied to Eve in the garden of Eden and manipulated her desire to know what God knows. He evoked lust within her heart and caused her to doubt the consequences of her actions because she had not known the meaning of death.

When Eve saw the beauty of the fruit and listened to the voice of the tempter, she reasoned that she should eat the fruit and gain the knowledge of God. Overcome by her desire and logic, she succumbed to the deception of the tempter and convinced Adam to do the same. *"And the serpent said unto the woman, Ye shall not surely die: For God doth know that in the day ye eat thereof, then your eyes shall be opened, and ye shall be as gods, knowing good and evil. And when the woman saw that the tree was good for food, and that it was pleasant to the eyes, and a tree to be desired to make one wise, she took of the fruit thereof, and did eat, and gave also unto her husband with her; and he did eat"* (Genesis 3:4-6).

The moment Adam gave in to the temptation to know what God knows; the moment of his disobedience, his nakedness was revealed. *"And the eyes of them both were opened, and they knew that they were naked..." (Genesis 3:7).* (The moment we disobey God, our nakedness is revealed.) Immediately Adam and Eve's eyes were opened, and the world as they knew it changed right in front of them. Instantly, they were consumed by Spiritual death and awakened to their carnality.

For the first time, they knew fear. They were afraid of what they saw in themselves and in each other and covered the beauty of the creation of their own bodies. (Something we are still doing today — covering ourselves physically, spiritually and emotionally from the beauty with which we were created.) They covered their internal nakedness (exposed sin) from God with external resources (fig leaves) believing that God would not see their sin. Albeit, to no avail because God sees all things. (Our sin causes us to seek covering in the presence of the Father. The blood of Jesus covers our sin, and the Father sees us through the Son.)

The consequences for giving in to the temptation to know what God knows was the beginning of man's suffering and sorrow. The fellowship between God and man was broken. That which God blessed and said was good, He now cursed. *"Unto the woman He said, I will greatly multiply thy sorrow and thy conception; in sorrow thou shalt bring forth children: and thy desire shall be*

97

Reverend Michele Taylor

to thy husband, and he shall rule over thee. "And unto Adam he said, Because thou hast harkened unto the voice of thy wife, and hast eaten of the tree, of which I commanded thee, saying, Thou shalt not eat of it: cursed is the ground for thy sake; in sorrow shalt thou eat of it all the days of thy life..." (Genesis 3:16-17).

God knew that once their eyes were opened, and their hunger for knowledge was exploited, their desire to be like God and live forever was inevitable. *"...and the Lord said, Behold, the man is become as one of us, to know good and evil: and now, lest he put forth his hand, and take also of the tree of life, and eat, and live forever. Therefore the Lord God sent him forth from the garden of Eden, to till the ground from whence he was taken...So He drove out the man; and He placed at the east of the garden of Eden Cherubims, and a flaming sword which turned every way, to keep the way of the tree of life" (Genesis 3:22 - 24).*

The very ground that once provided Adam and Eve with nourishment now carried the curse of man's sin. It would ultimately engulf their desecrated body and return it back from whence it came. *"...cursed is the ground for thy sake; in sorrow thou shalt eat of it all the days of thy life: Thorns, also and thistles shall it bring forth to thee; and thou shalt eat the herb of the field. In the sweat of thy face shalt thou eat bread, till thou return unto the ground; for out of it wast thou taken; for dust thou art, and unto dust shalt thou return" (Genesis 3:17).*

The earth groaned from the consequences of their sin, and the elements of nature turned against them. The mighty rivers bordering the garden of Eden now separated them from their home. (Sin separates us from our heavenly home.) They were strangers in a foreign land because they listened to Satan's lies. (Though we are children of Adam, we are yet strangers in a foreign land endeavoring to make it to our heavenly home.)

WHEN THE TEMPTER COMES

We don't purposely decide that "today I'm going to be tempted and succumb." There's no set time for the devil to tempt us. He does it at will. Sometimes the tempter comes when we are weak, and sometimes he comes when we are strong. When we are weak and vulnerable, he can slip in and do us in. When we feel strong, he can break us down with one indulgence. He is subtle, cunning, slick and evil. He's the master of his craft—Deception. He doesn't care who we are, what position we hold, how many degrees we have, or how long we've been saved. He's out to get us.

Look at how Satan tempted Jesus (our Lord and our Savior; the Redeemer of all mankind) when He was in the wilderness. The tempter came to Jesus trying to deceive Him in a moment of His physical weakness and vulnerability. *"And when the tempter came to him…"(Matthew 4:3).* He knew that Jesus was God, yet he still came. Satan challenged Christ's power and authority over His flesh. *"Command that these stones be made bread…."* *(Matthew 4:3).* Jesus was hungry, and His body was weak! All He had to do was speak the word and change the stones to bread. Jesus could have satisfied His hunger and fulfilled the desires of the flesh. He could have used His power and authority as God to provide for the longings of His flesh, but He didn't.

Jesus was challenged in His power and authority over all creation. *"Cast thyself down: for it is written, He shall give his angels charge concerning thee: and in their hands they shall bear thee up, lest at any time thou dash thy foot against a stone…"(Matthew 4:6).* It seemed to be the most logical thing to do. Certainly it made sense for Jesus to defy His physical boundaries and leap from one landing to another without the fear of falling or being consumed by the elements. After all, He could command the angels to carry His body to any location He desired. He was not in danger of losing His life (as it was not yet His time) because the angles would bring Him to safety and minister to His needs. Yet, He chose not to call upon the heavenly host. There was nothing He had to prove to the devil. (In His resistance to use His power, Jesus teaches us that we don't have to prove to the devil that we are powerful. He teaches us to preserve our energy and exercise our power and authority for matters that really count.)

The devil challenged Jesus' ownership. *"...again, the devil taketh him up unto an exceeding high mountain, and showeth him all the kingdoms of the world, and the glory of them: and saith unto him, All these things will I give thee, if thou wilt fall down and worship me..." (Mathew 4:8-9).* How bodacious of Satan to try to tempt Jesus with possessions that He already owned. Surely the devil believed that Jesus forgot His identity as God the Father, Jehovah, Yaweh, El Shaddai, Elohim and the great I AM. Surely the devil believes that we, too, forget our identity as the children of God—having all the rights and privileges bestowed upon us as joint heirs with Christ. How can he give to us an inheritance that is already ours?

If the devil tempted Jesus (God in the flesh), what will he try to do to you and me? To him, we are easy prey. He continues to use man's desire for power and authority as a weapon against us. We don't have to fall to the devil's tricks. We are made in God's image and are a reflection of God Himself. Jesus' experience in the wilderness is a great example of how we can resist any temptation the devil puts in front of us. He

101

showed us that we have the power and the authority to rebuke the devil and send him back to the pits of Hell. Yet, in our rebuke, we have to be careful and resist the temptation to *be* God, or assume His glory. That is the sin for which the devil is guilty. He disregarded the fact that he was the created, not the creator. In his boastfulness, self-exaltation and jealousy, he sought to *be* God. He wanted God's glory. We can't get so caught up and boastful in ourselves about God's power in us that we forget who we are in relation to the almighty Father. God is the creator, we are the created! (We can resist this temptation by obeying God, submitting our *will* to His *will* and by giving God His due honor and glory.)

ESCAPE WHILE YOU CAN

God always makes a way of escape. It's up to us to take it. As the redeemed, we have the power and authority to rebuke and resist the devil in the name of Jesus. This is our first line of defense. The spirit of God within us is always willing to resist temptation. However, the spirit is constantly at war with the flesh, and our desire to partake in the temptation. If we're not watchful to see the tempter when he comes (and the form in which he comes), we will yield.

Jesus instructed Peter to, *"Watch ye and pray, lest ye enter into temptation. The spirit is ready, but the flesh is weak" (Mark 14:38).* In this instruction and warning, Jesus reveals a way of escape and a method of prevention; Watch and Pray. When we watch and pray, we are more likely to see the temptations when they come, and we are better prepared to resist. The power of prevention is in our own *will. We* have to want to resist. We have to want to escape the temptation. Otherwise, our prayers are like the mouse running on a wheel and going nowhere. If we don't want to escape because we want to enjoy the temptation, we're wasting our time praying. If our heart desires to fulfill the pleasures of our flesh, we will ignore the voice of the Holy Spirit that convicts and warns us, and we will give in to the lust of our flesh. In this, we willingly accept the consequences of our actions.

JUST IN CASE

Having said this, I need to also say that there are times when we truly desire to resist temptation, but the temptation is too great for us to handle at that moment. Even in our attempt to rebuke the devil, we might give in to our weakness. Our human flaws kick in, and we find ourselves in a place where we don't want to be. The things we know not to do, we do anyway. We need to know that just in case we are overcome by temptation and sin, we don't have to stay there. James admonishes us to, *"Submit yourselves therefore to God. Resist the devil, and he will flee from you. Draw neigh to God, and He will draw neigh to you. Cleanse your hands, ye sinners; and purify your hearts, ye double minded. Be afflicted, and mourn, and weep: let your laughter be turned to mourning, and your joy to heaviness. Humble yourselves in the sight of the Lord, and He shall lift you up"* (James 4:7-10).

This formula is applicable in every situation of temptation. (1) Submit; give yourself to God completely. (2) Resist; turn away from the temptation. (3) Draw neigh; do what you have to do to get closer to God. (4) Cleanse and purify yourself; repent and ask God to forgive you. (5) Mourn; be sorrowful and mourn your actions and thoughts—grieve over your desire to sin. (6) Weep; exhibit a broken spirit and a contrite heart. (7) Show humbleness; exercise humility before God. Don't allow pride to keep you from repenting and seeking God's forgiveness.

Our healing lies in our willingness to repent and turn away from our sin. *"If my people, which are called by my name, shall humble themselves, and pray, and seek my face, and turn from their wicked ways, then will I hear from heaven, and will forgive their sin, and will heal their land"* (2 Chronicles 7:14). God will respond to our plea for forgiveness. He is just and forgiving. In His forgiveness, He will restore our broken relationship, renew our spirit and heal our land (our heart, our mind, our spirit and our soul).

TRUST GOD

Temptation comes as a trying of our faith. As long as we are trying to serve God, we will be tempted. We have to trust that God can and will deliver us no matter how great or small the temptation. We have to ask God to give us the power to resist. The power of God within us enables us to resist, if we choose to resist. Should we yield to the temptation, we can ask God to forgive us, and He will. (Try the forgiving nature of God. He proves Himself to be true to His Word every time.)

Trust that in every temptation, God is yet making us into powerful men and women of the Faith. He teaches us to trust solely in Him and His ability to keep us from falling. Soon we will come to know that the Lord is building our spiritual character and integrity. We will come to know that we must wait on the Lord to give us the desires of our heart rather than fulfill the lusts of our flesh. We will learn to wait with patience and to let patience have her perfect way within us. What a great joy it is to be tempted and to overcome.

I admonish you, trust that even if you yield to your temptation, God is willing to forgive you. Just repent and turn away from your sin. Don't allow yourself to stay in sin. The Lord wants to show you that if you seek His forgiveness, you will be forgiven, and your sins remembered no more. Through His love and loving chastisement, you will continue to grow in grace to a new level of spiritual maturity. Praise the Lord!

Reflections

1.   Do you remember the first temptation you were confronted with when you accepted Christ? What did you do?

2.   What was your most recent temptation? What did you do?

3.   What have you learned about God and yourself during your temptation and your deliverance?

4.   God is making you in the midst of the temptation. Allow Him to do this work in you. He will help you to overcome.

This is my prayer

"Count it all joy when ye fall into divers temptations; knowing this, that the trying of your faith worketh patience. But let patience have her perfect work, that ye may be perfect and entire wanting nothing" (James 1:2-3).

Lord, Save me from myself, the lust of my eyes and the desires of my flesh. Save me from disobedience, imaginations and corrupt thoughts, pre-meditated sin and deception. Help me to trust you, Lord, and never doubt your ability to deliver me from temptation.

Help me to watch and pray. Keep my eyes open so that I can see when the Tempter comes. Build a fortress of integrity in me so that my life reflects the image in which I was created. If I fall, please God, don't allow me to stay down. Give me a repentant heart so that I will always seek your face with humbleness and brokenness. My confidence is in you to restore me should I yield to temptation.

Thank you, Lord, for working your patience into me. Thank you for your saving grace and your keeping power. I bless you, Father, for keeping your hand upon me when the Tempter comes. Amen.

FIVE

BACKSLIDDEN AND RISEN
(Repentance, Resurrection and Restoration)

"He restoreth my soul...." (Psalm 23:3).

"For he saith to Moses, I will have mercy on whom I will have mercy, and I will have compassion on whom I will have compassion" (Romans 9:15).

"Brethren, if any of you do err from the truth, and one convert him; let him know, that he which converteth the sinner from the error of his way shall save a soul from death, and shall hide a multitude of sins" (James 5:19, 20).

"Having therefore these promises, dearly beloved, let us cleanse ourselves from all filthiness of the flesh and spirit, perfecting holiness in the fear of God" (2 Corinthians 7:1).

DEFINE BACKSLIDING, PLEASE

To Backslide is to turn away; to go back, to err, to be led astray, or seduced away. From a Christian perspective, it means to turn away from God, to go back to sin, to err from the Faith, to be seduced away from righteousness. Believers that backslide are seduced by demonic spirits and led away from the righteousness of God. The seduction, which often results in our yielding to various temptations, causes us to turn back to our sins.

We are introduced to the concept of Backsliding when the children of Israel were seduced away from God and turned to idol worship. Israel slowly erred from their belief in the unseen God of Abraham, Isaac and Jacob and relinquished their practice of separation and holiness. Israel lost faith in the God they could not see and touch, and they resorted to tangible ways of idol worship. Influenced by the worship patterns of pagan nations, Israel was enticed through the lust of their eyes and seduction of their flesh to abandon the almighty God and pursue the golden images of false deities.

Israel disobeyed God's law, rejected His commandments and turned its back to His love. Israel constantly rebelled against God and ignored His precepts. They were a people of defiance and rebellion. Even Moses, their deliverer and guide out of Egypt, learned quickly that the very people God chose to save from the hand of the oppressor were arrogant, defiant, rebellious and ungrateful. God called Israel stiff-necked. *"And the Lord said unto Moses, I have seen this people, and, behold, it is a stiff-necked people" (Exodus 32:9).* In Jeremiah, the Lord refers to Israel as backsliding children. *"....Oh backsliding children...." (Jeremiah 3:14).* Without a tight reign, Israel was easily led astray by their lust.

Israel's worship of false gods separated them from the true and living God. They willingly ignored God's law and engaged in spiritual intimacy with idols. The more Israel indulged in sin and disobedience, the further away they slid from being faithful to the God of their salvation. The further they slid away from God, the more they embraced idolatry. Each generation moved further away from the presence of God. Yet the Lord, who is never void of mercy and compassion, raised up a remnant that remained faithful.

The Lord sent prophets to deliver the message of salvation, restoration and reconciliation. Israel was given the opportunity to repent and be reconciled back to God; *"....Return, thou backsliding Israel, saith the Lord; and I will not cause mine anger to fall upon you; for I am merciful, saith the Lord, and I will not keep anger forever"* (*Jeremiah 3:12*).

The Lord promised to forgive Israel if they would admit their sins and transgressions; "*Only acknowledge thine iniquity, that thou hast transgressed against the Lord thy God, and hast scattered thy ways to the strangers under every green tree, and ye have not obeyed my voice, saith the Lord"* (*Jeremiah 3:13*). God assured His backslidden children, Israel, that He is married to them. He promised to blot out Israel's transgressions and restore the fidelity of the marriage if they returned to their first love and remained faithful.

God promised that those who returned to Him would receive the blessing of eternal life in the New Jerusalem. There, the ways of old would not be remembered; save the name of the Lord Jesus, the name that all nations will call upon. *"Turn, O backsliding children, saith the Lord; for I am married unto you: and I will take you one of a city, and two of a family, and I will bring you to Zion: and I will give you pastors according to mine heart, which shall feed you with knowledge and understanding. And it shall come to pass, when ye be multiplied and increased in the land, in those days, saith the Lord, they shall say no more, The ark of the covenant of the Lord; neither shall it come to mind: neither shall they remember it; neither shall they visit it; neither shall that be done any more. At that time they shall call Jerusalem the throne of the Lord; and all the nations shall be gathered unto it, to the name of the Lord, to Jerusalem; neither shall they walk anymore after the imagination of their evil heart" (Jeremiah 3:14-17).*

Because Israel rejected God, God rejected Israel and sought a new nation of Believers that would be faithful. Through the new covenant of Jesus Christ, the gentile was also given a right to salvation. We who believe in Jesus Christ as the Savior are among the new nation. (We are the chosen generation.) We have been adopted into the Body of Christ by our confession of faith and the infilling of the Holy Spirit. As Believers adopted into the royal family, we are included in the promise. God promises that because He is married to the backslider, should we backslide, we need only to repent and return to Him. If we return to Him, He will restore our broken fellowship, bless us and take us to our new home in Glory. God never goes back on His Word. His promises are our guarantee. Restoration is His promise, and our guarantee.

BACKSLIDING — A FORM OF REJECTION

When we turn away from God's love, we are telling Him that we no longer accept His divine plan and have found another way of life that pleases us more. When we reject God's love, we're telling God that we're tired of being called out and separated, and we desire to spiritually intermarry with idolaters. We're telling Him that the material things of this world have more value than our relationship with the Savior. We're telling God that we don't need Him. Truly, when we reject God's love, we have been led astray. We have been seduced by the harlots of Satan.

Perhaps it's not our intent to reject God's love. We don't mean to stray away from His love and the safety of His arms. However, when we are driven away by the lust of the flesh and led astray by false teachings that have come into the church, we err just enough to slowly lose sight of the Father. Our rejection of God's love manifests itself in our acts of rebellion and defiance. Slowly we slide away from the truth of God's Word, the fellowship of our church family, and the strength of our spiritual support systems. The further away we stray from God's Word, the easier it is to stay in sin. We find ourselves doing things we thought we would never do and going places we said we would never go.

We find ourselves believing that there's a better way to live than the way presented by the Church Body — according to our individual church experience. (Regardless of what we experience in church, there's no better way than God's way.) Then we justify our existence outside of our church family and often become angry when a church sister or brother confronts us about our backslidden condition. We are convinced that our attitude and actions towards the church and God's people are justified, but they're not.

We tend to believe that we are right in our way of thinking; when in reality, we're wrong. *"There is a way that seemeth right unto a man, but the end thereof are the ways of death…The backslider in heart shall be filled with his own ways…" (Proverbs 14:12,14).* Our heart hardens towards the things of God, and we become rebellious. Eventually, we willingly turn our back to the truth all together and reject the One who saved us.

HOW DOES ONE BACKSLIDE?

Backsliding is a condition that starts out with a small and undetected err, then progressively increases to a full straying away from God. Try walking on a straight line and deviate just one fraction of an inch. After awhile, you'll find yourself far away from your intended destination. The slightest err from the path creates another path that easily takes you completely off of the mark. Many of us have erred just a little bit and found ourselves disconnected from God. Some of us were so far away from holiness that it took a long time to get back on track. Like Israel, we slid away from our first love and pursued the lustful desires of our flesh. We danced with temptation and were seduced into accepting the ways of the ungodly. God separated us unto Himself in holiness and righteousness, yet we wandered into the land of idol worship.

There are several ways in which one can backslide. The most common and identifiable manifestation of backsliding is seen when someone leaves a church. When a person leaves a church, it is not always because they intentionally want to backslide and walk away from God; neither is it a clear indicator that they are out of love with the Father. Rather, they have fallen out of love with God's people and reject the ways of the Church as an organization. Something someone did or said turned them away from a church. More often than not, if you ask someone why they left their church, they will tell you that someone hurt them, the leadership did something that disturbed them and they no longer trust that leadership, they don't like the church's politics or drastic changes in the direction of their church, or that something occurred that caused them to become so outraged that they couldn't stay any longer. What started out as a small tolerable pain progressively intensified and developed into full-blown hurt. (Sometimes the damage is irrevocable.) Hurt turns into anger and anger turns into rage. Because most Believers try not to display violence, their rage gets expressed in defiance and rebellion.

When Believers leave their church, we believe that we are "leaving a church," not God. We usually join another church, or religious movement, in order to stay connected to God. Herein lies the problem with church-hopping. The attitude from being hurt and having unresolved issues from one church follows us to the next church and the next and the next. We may find ourselves being hurt in every church we attend, yet we continue to move on to the next church looking for the "perfect church." (Which, by the way, does not exist.)

The core of our pain was never rooted out and dealt with. The fight or flight defense mechanism arises within us to protect our heart and emotions. The wall of arrogance, indifference and callousness gets built higher and higher with each suppressed hurt and each new hurt. The wall is built so high and so thick that nothing can get over it, around it or through it. It is an impenetrable fortress. The heart of flesh is hardened into a heart of stone. Rebellion and defiance sets in, and the simple act of leaving a church potentially turns into leaving the Faith all together.

Spiritual complacency is another way Believers backslide. While those who remain in the Church Body may appear to be in fellowship with other Believers, we are not. Our physical body may be in the House of God, but our heart and spirit have left the building.

Spiritually, the complacent Believer is in the same state of brokenness as the Believer who leaves the church—physically. Our sins are often undetected by the natural eye, and we can be so complacent and comfortable in our sin that we do nothing about it. We believe all is well and never see the need to repent. Rather, we continue to serve on the usher board, sing in the choir, preach the gospel, give tithes and offering and say Amen on point without asking for forgiveness. We become comfortable with our superficial worship and orchestrated praise; and, our service in the church tends to be merely the fulfillment of well-developed habits and ritualistic traditional practices. We are task oriented and functional rather than divinely inspired to work the works of the One who saved us. Our motives for doing anything in the House of God are diverted from being God-centered to being self-centered or people-centered. We turn away from glorifying God and turn towards seeking glory for ourselves.

Complacency causes us to go along with the program without putting forth any effort to seek the *will* of God, or the truth of God. We don't question what we see and hear. We straddle the fence when it comes to important matters concerning the business of the church, and we are indecisive in our actions. We are either double-minded or indifferent. All Hell can break loose around us; and we don't care, or we don't take a stand. We feel that certain matters don't really concern us, or affect us personally. Therefore we don't need to get involved, and an "I don't care" attitude seeps into everything we do.

We've stopped talking to God and communing with the Holy Spirit. It's an effort to clap our hands when a spirit-filled song is sung by the choir. We fall asleep when we close our eyes during prayer time. We stop hearing the preached Word and daydream about what we're going to do when we leave the service. The Holy Spirit is moving, and we're looking around hoping that the Believers will stop dancing so we can finish and go home. Our heart is hardened to the things of God, and we're only coming to church because that's what we do. In our complacency, we've quietly fallen away from our place in God. We've backslidden in our heart and don't even know it.

Some of us have backslidden because of our misplaced affections for leadership. We idolize our leaders and love them more than we love the Lord. Our adoration and affections towards leadership have us trapped in idolatry. Our need for approval causes us to slide away from worshipping God in order to seek the approval of leadership. We are seduced into worshipping our leaders because we can see them, and they give us the open praise and attention we desire. Male and female alike, we do it. We want to be acknowledged by our pastor, our bishop, our overseer and each other. Our motives for doing service in the House of the Lord tends to get lost between our commitment to serving God, and our desire to please man.

God is a jealous God and will not tolerate the adoration that is due Him being given to man. We were created to worship God, not man. We were created to glorify God, not to seek glory for ourselves from man. Misplaced affections cause us to slide away from our first love. Like Israel, God will abase the false gods that set themselves before God's people like a brazen altar. God will tear down the altar of false worship no matter what form it takes including pastors, bishops, overseers and the like.

Some Believers backslide because we are angry with God. We lost a loved one, or don't understand why God would allow so many bad things to happen to us. We are led away from God because the evil one tricked us into believing that God doesn't love us. If He did, why would He let certain things happen? A Believer that's tricked into believing that God doesn't love them is vulnerable to being tricked into blaspheming the Holy Spirit. To blaspheme the Holy Spirit is an unpardonable sin. *"Verily I say unto you, All sins shall be forgiven unto the sons of men, and blasphemies wherewith soever they shall blaspheme: But he that shall blaspheme against the Holy Ghost hath never forgiveness, but is in danger of eternal damnation" (Mark 3:28-29).* God and His spirit are one in the same. To curse the Holy Spirit is to curse God. To curse God is guaranteed eternal death. No one can curse God and live eternally in His kingdom.

IN OR OUT

In or out of the Church Body; whether physically removed from the building and the Faith, or in our heart and spirit, we have strayed away from God. Whether willfully or by seduction, we've turned our back to God's face. This is a serious condition to be in. If we deny God, He will deny us. Whether we're in or out of the church building, we are out of fellowship with God. Though His mercy endures forever; and His grace saves us, the relationship with the Father is broken and needs to be restored. God doesn't have to shine His face upon us ever again.

Thanks be to God, whose mercy is from everlasting to everlasting, for repentance and restoration.

I was both in and out of the church; willfully and seductively out of the *will* and fellowship of God, but His mercy endured. I experienced the process of slowly erring from the straight and narrow path of righteousness, and I found myself far removed from God's presence. I turned my back on God and all that He had purposed for my life. I denied Him, rejected Him and rejected His people. I lost total focus on being saved, what I was saved from and what I was saved for. I forgot my promise, my vow and my commitment to God. In my heart, I said that I was finished with the Church, and God's people. I didn't want to have any part of it, or those people that claimed to be saved. I told God, He could have it!

What I didn't understand at the time was the power of the seal of redemption. The words "He'll never leave me or forsake me" were not yet real in my life. I was so busy trying to run away from God, that I didn't realize how His hands were holding me in place. I didn't realize how His breath kept my spirit from dying completely. The Lord knew what was really going on in my heart. He knew that I was only responding to being hurt by my church family, and that I was expressing my anger the only way I knew how. God knew that I didn't mean what I said, and that I would one day repent and return unto Him.

The day of my restoration was preordained and waiting to be fulfilled. God knew that I'd be sitting here today writing this testimony that He restored my soul. For *the making of you* in my life, this day was declared in the heavens before the very foundation of the earth was lain. I know that God can and will restore the backslidden Believer because one day, He restored my soul and renewed His spirit within me. (Unto His own glory.)

THREE STRIKES

Strike One: Spiritual immaturity. I couldn't handle the weight and pressure that came along with the responsibilities I had as a Church Administrator. I was on the inside (the inner circle) and was sworn to confidentiality about everything I knew about every member. I had become self-righteous and judgmental because of what I knew. I was exposed to the political dirt behind church business, and the subtle spiritual seductions of leadership. I silently carried in my heart the weight of the knowledge of the sins of the church. Having suffered persecution early in my saved journey and having risen above several experiences with "church hurt," I thought I was spiritually mature. Through a few more experiences, I found out that I needed to grow a bit more. I was still a babe and had a long way to grow.

The church I attended had undergone a major shift in leadership, and the church members were divided in their loyalty. This was just one of several "church splits" I had known and experienced in my lifetime. The separation left many of the members vulnerable. Some of the members left the church, and the members that stayed tried to keep the church functioning. In my own vulnerability, I was dysfunctional in my duties and very despondent. Yet, I stayed for another two years because I had no where else to go.

Another shift came, and my church experienced a wave of covert spiritualism and witchcraft. God gifted me with spiritual discernment and the ability to see angels and demons. However, the more I tried to point out the demons I saw, the more I was persecuted. Satanic rituals were performed under the guise of the Holy Spirit, and familiar and seducing spirits continued to thrive unchallenged. At a particular service, one of the spiritualist cursed me out because I would not allow her to lay hands on me during prayer. (That was my cue to leave the church.) I wasn't spiritually mature enough to stand and fight the spiritual battle alone. I felt hurt because leadership did not believe what I saw and knew to be the truth about the demonic forces that had infiltrated the church. I felt the need to escape an environment of witchcraft that I knew all too well. (The gifts of the Holy Spirit will not operate in a house that rejects them.)

Strike Two: A love gone wrong. I left my church and joined a youth crusade. We were singing and ministering and having a good time in the Lord. I felt rejuvenated and alive. All I wanted to do was sing for Jesus. Then I fell in love with one of the members. We had a great relationship, a great friendship and we were bonded in the spirit. I was convinced that we would be together for life. Then trouble came, and the relationship ended. I was grief-stricken and overwhelmed with hurt. I tried to continue singing with the crusade, but my emotions got the best of me. I could no longer sing in his presence and pretend that everything was just fine. My heart couldn't take the pain of being around him without being with him, so I left the crusade.

Strike Three: Great expectations. Shortly after leaving the crusade, I experienced another church hurt that caused me to declare that I wanted nothing else to do with "those people." I was working for a religious institute at the time, and was doing quite well. A shift came in my personal and spiritual life, and I experienced yet another deep hurt. Still working through my inner turmoil from past hurts, the new situation compounded the hurt.

In short, I had undergone surgery to remove a large tumor behind my pelvic bone. The healing process kept me out of work for a month. My boyfriend (a minister) only visited me once; a very small contingency of co-workers communicated with me, and since I left my church, none of the Saints came to visit either. With all that I had done in my own church; all of the Christians and religious leaders I knew; and all of the ministers, pastors, elders and missionaries I had fellowshipped with, I still felt abandoned. I didn't understand how my boyfriend, the minister, didn't want to see me in my infirmed condition. I didn't understand how my church leaders didn't call me to find out if I needed anything...not even to pray with me. It bewildered me when I later learned that my constituents from the religious institute didn't know that I was infirmed, but were told that I resigned. It hurt me to know how insignificant I really was in the lives of the people I loved so much, and in the community of Christian Believers that I served.

I was angry with God and God's people. In my anger and despair, the spirit of rebellion gripped me like an octopus that wraps its tentacles around its prey...spewing out poisonous fluids that deaden the nervous system and renders its victims completely helpless. I told God that I had enough; I was finished, and I didn't want to have any part of the church or church folk! My heart was hardened, my spirit was vexed and my mind was made up. There was nothing anyone could say or do that would have convinced me that I would ever set foot in the church again.

My spirit died on the day I told God, "You Got it!" I broke my vow and the fellowship with the Father. The *will* to live for Christ died, and my desire to minister to God's people died as well. Satan deceived me into believing that the fruit of temptation was more desirable than the fruit of the spirit. He played on my humanness, distorted the truth about every hurtful situation, blinded my eyes from God's love and planted rebellion in my heart. My mind was seduced away from God, and I slid back into sin by the lust of the flesh. My rebellion against God, and my rejection of His people was a direct rejection of God in me, and His *will* for my life.

I rebelled against being a servant of the most high God. The gifts imparted into my spirit for the edification of the Body of Christ lay dormant and were subject to demonic influence. Indirectly, I told God that I refused to be a witness, I refused to spread the gospel, I refused to teach His Word and impart revelation knowledge. I refused to sing praises to His glory. I refused to write according to His inspiration. I refused to show kindness and compassion to His beloved people. I refused to heal the sick by the laying on of hands, and the emotionally sick by giving Godly counsel — the list goes on. In my actions, I was telling God that He would not get the glory out of my life. Like Israel, I was lost in the wilderness and forgot about the God who saved me.

KEPT BY THE HOLY SPIRIT

In my backslidden condition, the Lord allowed me to exercise my own *will*. While Satan danced emphatically thinking that he won, God was preparing my deliverance. My saving grace was that I did not blaspheme the Holy Spirit. Though I was in a backslidden condition, I had not belligerently cursed the Holy Spirit. I hadn't completely lost my mind! (Thank you Jesus!) God was present in my unconscious mind. I simply chose not to listen to His voice when He whispered, "Repent." Though the Holy Spirit would nudge me, and I'd feel convicted, I didn't repent. In the meantime, the Holy Spirit kept me from extremities. Yes, I took on some old habits and indulged in some familiar sins, but the Holy

Spirit kept me from a reprobate mind. Though my behavior had gone to the left of God's Word, and sometimes to the far far left, the Holy Spirit reminded me of a scripture or a song, and caused my heart to feel His presence. Through the Word of God hidden in my heart, I knew that God was still God.

Finally, in my sin, I reached a point where I acknowledged that the Holy Spirit was dealing with me. I knew I had strayed far from the *will* of the Lord, and I wanted to get back into His grace. But I didn't want to deal with the Church Body. Other situations arose that intensified my need to escape from the presence of evil and from my own inner turmoil. Wanting to get away from an environment of sin, I loaded everything I owned into a rental truck and moved out of state with a friend. I knew that wasn't the real answer to my backslidden condition, but I hoped it would suffice. Oh yes, I knew that repentance was the way out of my sin, however, I was not ready or willing to repent.

Then, in what I call my "great escape," I found myself alone in a motel room with only one change of clothing, some basic toiletries, loose change in my wallet, and a credit card. I stayed in the motel for two weeks alone—deliberating. The money was running out, and every few days I had to pay the motel in order to stay longer. The cashier knew something was wrong, but as long as I paid my bill, there was no problem. My hunger pangs were satisfied by 7-Eleven nachos, hot dogs and coffee. Snow was on the ground, and the town was at a stand still—nothing was moving, not even a snow plow.

One morning, just about 6 A.M., I was lying in bed when the spirit of the Lord spoke to my heart. "This is not what I have for you." I knew it was the voice of the Lord. My conscious mind responded, and I whispered, "This is not what God has for me." The Holy Spirit suppressed deep within my soul interceded on my behalf. He presented my case to the Son, and the Son presented it to the Father. Jesus advocated for me in the heavenly courts and pleaded my fate. The Father looked at me through the blood of Jesus and declared mercy upon my soul. The Holy Spirit spoke expressly to my heart concerning God's *will* in my life. God's *will* touched my true desire, and my true desire touched the *will* of my heart. My heart was convicted, and my soul repented. The Holy Spirit kept me until I repented.

RESURRECTION AND RESTORATION

I was alone with God in the silence of the dawn pleading for the restoration of my soul. The

130

same Lord I rejected was the same Lord I called upon with a broken spirit and contrite heart— tears seeping into the gully of my pillow. I opened my mouth and whispered, "Lord I'm sorry. Please forgive me." I didn't have to verbalize the details of my sin, nor the issues that caused me to slide out of God's *will*. I acknowledged my sin, and I repented.

Immediately, the Holy Spirit commanded me to get up. Straight away, I got out of the bed and out of my backslidden condition. When I put my foot on the floor and stood up, I stood up into a new life—a resurrected life. I called my sister, explained to her the situation and asked her if I could stay with her until I got back on my feet. I checked out of the motel, took a taxi to the bus station and headed home. My sister welcomed me with open arms, and my nephew offered to let me sleep in his room. The next day, I took care of my banking and other business, and signed up with a temporary employment agency. Within two days, I was working. In my shame, I didn't tell my parents or my dearest friends all that I had been through—only that I was home.

Angered by the change in me, the devil went on a war path. He tried to kill me several times. Once, I was hit by a car and knocked to the ground. I jumped up, shook myself off and kept walking. The driver was devastated, and I had to calm her down by assuring her that there were no injuries. The same night, I attended a worship service and testified about what God had done. Though I was not ready to share the details, I declared that the Lord restored my soul (Psalm 23:2). I cried unto the Lord, and He washed my soul. He cleansed my heart and renewed His spirit within me. The praises went up, and God was glorified.

The Lord assured me that I belonged to Him and was on the road to spiritual healing. I was not ready to join a church, however, I knew that what I needed could only be received in the fellowship with the Saints of God. Finally, I took membership with a church that I learned to call "home." I lay before the Lord in total submission learning His statutes. I humbly submitted myself to God's *will* by the simple declaration of, "Yes Lord." "Yes Lord" was not the conclusive chant used when the preacher came up to deliver the Word of God, or the interlude from one part of the service to another. For me, it was a personal declaration of submission and obedience to the God of my salvation.

During my restoration, the Lord taught me forgiveness. He rooted out the bitterness from my heart, and restored the love for God's people within me. My spirit was renewed, and my joy restored. The Holy Spirit stirred up the spiritual gifts within me, and made me a warrior for spiritual warfare. The Holy Spirit resurrected in

132

me the call to ministry and my desire to serve. I was compelled to witness to Christians whose experience with church hurt caused them to backslide. The Lord used my experience of renewal to bring hope to the fallen and despondent Believer. He made me a living epistle, *"....not written with ink, but with the spirit of the living God; not in tables of stone, but in fleshly tables of the heart"* (2 Corinthians 3:2). God be glorified.

Those of us who have been restored to the Faith have an obligation to bring restoration to others that have fallen. *"Brethren, if any of you do err from the truth, and one convert him; Let him know, that he which converteth the sinner from the error of his way shall save a soul from death, and shall hide a multitude of sins"* (James 5:19-20).

HEAL THE LAND

I've taken this time to share with you a very personal event in my Christian walk because I care about your soul. In restoring me to the Faith, the Lord restored and increased my love for His people. He gave me a charge to proclaim healing to the backslider. I know what it is to be out of the *will* of God and how difficult it is to come back to the Lord; and to the Church Body. However, the experience God allowed me to have reinforced that we who are the redeemed of the Lord are sealed by the Holy Spirit until the second coming of our Lord Jesus Christ. Through repentance, the Lord will restore us and renew His spirit within us.

God is a God of mercy and compassion. He is able and willing to forgive us and receive us back into the fold. As with Israel, He will declare, *"I will heal their backsliding, I will love them freely: for mine anger is turned away from them"* (Hosea 14:7). When we return to the Lord, He will heal the desert land of our soul and renew His spirit within us. God's unconditional love breathes life into a dead and dying nation. There is a nation of backsliders (fallen believers seduced away from God's love and service) that are yearning to be healed.

The Lord is just and true to His Word. He is waiting patiently to send healing into the land. He is longing for their return. He is calling them one by one by the voice of His spirit speaking to their hearts telling them to come home (as He called me). Herein lies the command for the backslider: Do your first work over. *"Remember from whence thou art fallen, and repent, and do the first works..." (Revelation 2:5).*

If you are one to whom the Holy Spirit now speaks, harden not your heart when you hear His voice. *"Wherefore as the Holy Ghost saith, today if ye will hear His voice, harden not your hearts..."*

(Hebrews 3:7-8). This is your opportunity to begin a renewed life in Christ. Repent and start all over again. It's not too late. The Lord will receive you and heal you of your backslidden condition. In your own resurrection, God is making you into a living testimony. Receive His restoration.

Reflections

1. Are you a backslider? If you are, this is your time for spiritual restoration. God is calling you to come home. You are that lost sheep that Jesus came to find. You are the beloved of God, and He is looking for your return. Repent and come home. The Lord is waiting just for you.

2. So you don't want to go back to "that church." You don't have to. There's a church where you fit in. No one knows your past or your present. You can have a new beginning in a new land. Let the Lord direct your path to that place of fellowship.

3. I know you've been hurt, but it's time to get over it. God has a work for you to do—my sister and my brother. Rise up and do the work that you were called to do.

This is my prayer

"Blessed is he whose transgression is forgiven, whose sin is covered. Blessed is the man unto whom the Lord imputeth not iniquity, and in whose spirit there is no guile....I acknowledge my sin unto thee, and mine iniquity have I not hid. I said, I will confess my transgressions unto the Lord; and thou forgavest the iniquity of my sin" (Psalm 32: 1-2, 5).

There is no sin hidden from you, Oh Lord. I admit that I have sinned and fallen short of your glory. I turned my back on you. I've ignored your precepts. I've dishonored your calling in my life. Please forgive me. Take me back and restore my faith. Raise me with your right hand and renew your spirit within me. Heal my desert land. I rejoice in your resurrection. I rejoice in the resurrection of my soul. I gladly speak of your mercies made known to me. Thou art divine; the giver of life. You breathed life into my dying spirit. Praises be to God in the highest. Praises to the God of mercy. Amen

SIX

TRAVAILING TO TRIUMPH
(Overcoming Power)

"Thine, O Lord, is the greatness, and the power, and the glory, and the victory, and the majesty: for all that is in the heaven and in the earth is thine; thine is the kingdom, O Lord, and thou art exalted as head above all. Both riches and honour come of thee, and thou reignest over all; and in thine hand is power and might; and in thine hand it is to make great and to give strength unto all. Now therefore, our God, we thank thee, and praise thy glorious name"
(I Chronicles 29:11-13).

"O clap your hands, all ye people, shout unto God with the voice of triumph. For the Lord most high is terrible; he is a great King over all the earth" (Psalm 47:1).

THE MOUNTAIN-TOP EXPERIENCE

I love the mountains! They proclaim the majesty of God! Every chance I get to travel to the mountains, I'm there. The first time I realized that I loved mountains, I was traveling through the mountains of Arizona. The awesomeness of their size embraced my spirit as the mountain range towered along the roadside on the left and the right. The red compacted clay was a sight I had never seen before. I'd only seen such splendor in pictures, and now I was privileged to observe the view first hand.

Some years later, I had the pleasure of taking a trip to Shenandoah Valley, Virginia, right in the heart of the Blue Ridge Mountains. A beautiful view of the mountain range could be seen from every side of the hotel where I stayed. Although it was a wonderful sight, it was no comparison to what I saw during my mountain top experience. My life was changed forever. Right after breakfast one morning, the group I traveled with set out on a field trip. We drove upward around the mountain's edge. We came to a rest stop and took a few minutes to take in the view. The scenery was breath-taking! Then the real journey began. From that point, we hiked about an hour's journey. Finally, we came out of the wooded area and were approaching a clearing. As we reached

139

the clearing, all that my eyes could see was the vastness of God's glory. We reached the top of the mountain and were standing at the very edge of the peak. Oh my God! Awesome!

There were mountains everywhere I looked. I could see the valley below, the road we had just traveled and a small river (at least it looked small from where I was standing). The trees were perfectly groomed. Their leaves created the most picturesque landscape I had ever seen. There were hues of burnt orange, deep scarlet, sunburst yellow, forest green and chocolate brown for miles and miles. I inhaled the crisp, fresh air and swooned from its intoxicating aroma. As I stood there looking over the edge (praying that I wouldn't fall), I stretched out my arms and embraced the presence of God. I felt like Moses when he looked over the mountains and saw the promised land. Tears streamed down my face, and the Holy Spirit endowed me with His presence.

I had become one with Moses, one with creation and one with God. In that moment, I realized how blessed I was to be standing there. God allowed me to see Him in the splendor of His creation; and, He allowed me to see myself in relation to the grandeur of His creation. I was humbled by His greatness, His power, His might and His majesty. I felt my continence change as God spoke to my spirit. There, on the mountain top, I received His instructions to "Go and tell." To see the splendor of God's creation from a view point high above civilization is a humbling experience. Yet to hear God's voice while gazing upon the beauty of the artistry of His creation was even more humbling.

The freshness of the mountain air saturated the density of my consciousness. The whispering winds carried the weight of my troubled soul far into the atmosphere, and my spirit was healed by the release. Now when I'm in need of emotional, mental and spiritual refreshing, I escape to the mountains. I know that I will meet God in that familiar place where He changed my life. I know that I will hear a Word from the Lord every time. So I'm constantly seek opportunities to embrace a spiritual renewal in a place where I can receive a touch from the Lord without the intrusion of external affairs. There, on the mountain top, I can envision the wings of angels as they soar over the highest peaks and into the heavens. Beneath their wings, I find peace.

THE CLIMB

To get to the top of any mountain, you have to climb. Unless you're air-lifted or carried, you have to climb. How you climb makes the difference of how you arrive. If you climb with a bad attitude because you don't want to exert yourself or get dirty, you won't appreciate the nuances of the climb or your arrival. You'll feel imposed upon to have to climb in the first place. Then you'll feel appalled that you had to struggle, sweat and subject your body to the intense physical strain. You'll feel as though you could have taken another route, a mini-van, a jeep or a helicopter. On the other hand, you can climb eagerly even though you know that it won't be easy, and you may even stumble and fall. When you climb with the anticipation of reaching the top, you'll prepare yourself mentally, emotionally and physically for whatever you might encounter as you ascend. When you reach the top, you'll experience victory.

So it is with every challenge that we face in our spiritual lives. God challenges us to climb, but He doesn't always tell us how. He leaves it to us to adjust our attitude so that we can appreciate the experience. The Lord expects us to prepare ourselves, to the best of our ability, so that we can overcome the obstacles and struggles we'll encounter along the way. He trusts that we will get up, should we fall, and keep going. He depends on us to help those that are climbing with us, along side of us, in front of us or behind us so that we all reach the top, even if our individual pace and abilities are different.

God expects us to climb (out of despair, depression, self-indulgence, self-righteousness, etc). He equips and empowers us to climb. He helps us to climb, and He comforts us during the climb. The Lord directs our path and provides light through the darkness along the way. He moves some obstacles and gives us strength and knowledge to overcome others. The Lord provides for our every need and protects us from the dangers that lurk around hidden places. He lifts us up when we get discouraged, and He builds in us endurance and fortitude to withstand every test.

Why do we climb? We climb because we have to. We climb because we want to have a peak experience with God. We endure hardship because we want to see His face in glory. We sustain bruises because we know that healing comes when we complete the journey. We suffer persecution and criticism because we know that our reward awaits us when we see Jesus; the King of Kings, and Lord of Lords. We climb to have victory over the enemy. We climb to be triumphant.

THE PROCESS

We are victorious because we are in Christ, and Christ is in us. Nevertheless, we have to travail in order to be triumphant. Travail is not a voluntary action. No one really wants to go through pain and hardship. We'd rather not deal with adversity, struggles and conflict if we don't have to. Do you remember the last time you volunteered to go into the lion's den? (See my point?!)

Daniel didn't volunteer to go into the Lion's Den and sit amongst the hungry lions. He was thrown into the pit against his *will*. The adversary expected Daniel to be devoured by the lions, but Daniel trusted God to deliver him. His experience with the God of Abraham gave him the assurance that God would deliver him, if He *willed* it to be so. Daniel's faith had been tested in many other moments of travailing, and now his faith prevailed. Even if God did not deliver him, Daniel knew that God was able. Daniel trusted God, and God responded to Daniel's trust in Him.

We are often thrown into the lion's den against our *will*, and our faith is tested. Every adversity teaches us to pray a little harder, longer or differently. Through the process of being delivered, we learn who God is in our lives and to trust Him for our deliverance. We learn that the Lord hears our every cry and supplication, and He is faithful to answer. When we call upon the Father, in the name of Jesus, He will answer. Our relationship with the King of Kings is fortified, and we gain strength to endure the next test. We receive strength to stand strong in our faith; and not bend with every wind of doctrine, or give in and give up when the adversary raises his ugly head.

Process helps us to understand the relationship between our suffering and Christ's suffering on the cross. (If we suffer with Christ, we shall also reign with Him.) Process teaches us the importance and value of suffering. Process helps us to grow into spiritual maturity as we learn to endure and overcome. It helps us to develop agility and flexibility in our Christian walk. Without process, we tend to become spiritually inept and stagnant. Where there's no process, there's no growth.

STEP BY STEP

Just as the steps for growth in the natural, our Christian walk is a step by step process. Each step takes us closer to appreciating victory when we've reached the pinnacle of our situation and overcome. Daniel's faith was strengthened with each adverse situation he travailed against and triumphed over. He was able to face each new adversity with the assurance that God is a triumphant deliverer. The process of being delivered increased his faith in God's ability to deliver him. Every time the Lord delivers us from adversity, our faith increases. We come to know that if the Lord *wills*, He will deliver us. We can trust Him to do that. But if He doesn't, we still know that He is able because He's God, and He's done it before.

Why: Why, Lord, am I going through this problem? Why am I having so much trouble? Why am I standing still? Why are they on my case all the time? Why me? God has a purpose for our lives. In order to fulfill that purpose, He has to mold and shape us into what and who He wants us to be. We have to be purified and cleansed of the character flaws that hold us back from fulfilling the *will* of God in us. If we keep this in the forefront of our mind, the process of travailing to triumph will be easier to understand. The "Why" step is one we won't have to go through every time we encounter suffering because we already know the answer to the question. Why? Because God is shaping us into usable vessels for a divine purpose in His divine plan. We are instruments the Lord will use to exemplify His delivering power.

How: How, Lord, will you deliver me from this pit? There are barricades surrounding the perimeter of my circumstances, and spikes lodged into the walls that prick my flesh every time I kick at them and try to get out? How, Lord, will you raise me up when I am pressed down so low? While we concern ourselves with how God will deliver us, God has already designed a plan for our deliverance. The way of escape has already been prepared and is in the implementation phase. We cannot speculate or choose how God will deliver us. That's really not our business. He's God, and He can do what He wants to do, when He wants to do it and how He wants to do it. If God chooses to allow trouble and turmoil in our lives, that's His right as our Father and our creator. We need to understand that God's way is perfect, and His thoughts are pure. Whatever God does in our lives, and with our lives, is planned with perfection for the edification of the Body of Christ. It is His *will* and good pleasure to work His perfect plan in us. How the Lord chooses to work His plan of deliverance is also His good pleasure. (It pleases God when we exercise our faith. It pleases Him when we trust in His ability to deliver us, regardless of how He does it.)

What: Once we learn to trust that how God will deliver us is for our own perfection and the edifying of the Body of Christ, we will stop asking Him, "How?" and begin asking ourselves,

147

"What?" What will we do when God does what He does? In the conversion story of Saul to Paul, the Lord told Saul that It is hard to kick against the pricks. He tells us the same thing when we try to avoid the travailing process and rush to be triumphant. Kicking against the pricks is like going against the grain; it's rough! When we follow the path and direction wherein the Lord leads us, we will obtain peace. However, if we fight against His designated path, we're fighting against our own peace — and peace will not be obtained. We're hurting ourselves and making the process longer and more painful than it has to be.

I strongly suggest that when we know there are spikes (obstacles) that can prick us (hurts us), stop kicking. Stop fighting against what God is doing in us (because we don't like the process) and stand still so that we can see the salvation of the Lord. When we're standing still, we can hear the silence that beckons our spirit. In the silence, God speaks. His voice directs us to look at obstacles as tools for deliverance rather than as annoying hindrances that distract our focus. When we stand still for a moment, the Holy Spirit will change our perspective and cause us to rethink the process. He will inspire us to use the obstacle as a step-ladder to climb up and out of our situation and into victory. Every weapon formed against us becomes a tool for deliverance.

When we rethink the "What" question of the process of travailing to triumph, we will remember that the Lord is our fortress, and He sets up barricades to protect us from dangers seen and unseen. It's His way of keeping us safe from the dangers lurking around our situation. Instead of convincing ourselves that the walls around us are a barricade to keep us in, think of them as the protection of the Lord keeping danger out. Consider how they protect our soul and spirit from destruction. As we stand still in the safety of the Lord, we can observe the dangers around us and determine when it's safe to proceed. We may even find that it's better to stay in the safety of the pit for a season until the situation clears.

Sometimes we just have to wait things out in the dark; in that place of uncertainty where our faith takes precedence. By faith, God will teach us how to wait in the dark, and He will teach us patience in our waiting. We may need to learn how to wait on the Lord so that we don't miss out on what He is saying and doing in and through our lives. While we're waiting in the darkness of the belly of despair, the Lord will remind us that He is the light. All we need to do is walk towards the light. While we're in the pit, we may have to breathe in the stench of our own sin in order to understand that our sin presents an offensive odor to our Lord. Then, maybe we'll appreciate the sweet fragrance of deliverance. We may have to endure the coldness of isolation and being forgotten before we can appreciate the bliss of liberation.

Perhaps the Lord is showing us that there's a different way for deliverance than what we anticipated. Like Joseph, God may send a stranger—an unlikely person—who will have compassion for our situation and drop a rope into the pit to pull us up to safety. Perhaps the Lord is showing us His compassion so that we will have compassion for others. Whatever it is the Lord wants us to learn in this process of suffering to obtain victory, we have a chance to examine ourselves.

Self-examination will bring us back to the question, "What?" What, Lord, would you have me to do? What is it, Lord, that I'm not doing or need to do? Did I miss the mark? Am I going about this in my own way and ignoring your voice? What do I need to do to consecrate myself, rededicate myself and sanctify myself again so that I can be used by you? What, Lord, should I be paying attention to? What is my attitude? Where is my commitment?

We have to see our own attitude and actions in the midst of our going through and come to grips with how our actions and acceptance of responsibility (or lack of) play a vital role in our deliverance. Then we can focus on doing what we need to do to overcome the obstacles that are keeping us from being triumphant.

TRIUMPH TAKES RESILIENCE

Resilience is the ability to spring back into shape. It's having the strength to recover; to handle the situation. Resilience is having buoyancy; the ability to rise back to the top when we've been pushed to the bottom. No matter how bent out of shape we get from a situation, the Holy Spirit gives us resilience to bounce back and straighten out. Being able to pull ourselves back together (with the help of the Lord) after being stretched out to the limit, is a sign of overcoming power. When we can pick ourselves up after being pushed down, weighted down, knocked down, held down and held back, squashed, kicked, sat down and sat on, we show God that we're determined to hold on to His unchanging hands. We show the devil that we're not going to accept everything he dishes out; neither are we going into a hole to hide.

Resilience exemplifies our trust in God. We trust God to take us through, to deliver us, to lift us up, to show us the way, to guide us and to give us the victory. We trust that God allows all things to happen for a reason, and that reason is always

for our good. He has a divine purpose for our going through whatever it is we go through. Therefore, we trust Him to give us the strength and the *will* to endure. God's Spirit compels us to get up and brush ourselves off. He bends us back into shape and helps us to adapt to the changes that have occurred. We are resilient because God made us resilient—pliable, adaptable and flexible—so that we can spring back from adversity with overcoming power.

A TIME TO REJOICE

We made it to the top of our situation and can look over into the promised land of victory. We now have experience and the assurance that God is a deliverer. We know that our help comes from the Lord, and we know how to call upon His name when we need His help. We've overcome doubt and fear, and our attitude is different. We can rethink the process of our suffering and use the obstacles in front of us as stepping stones to higher ground. We learned to have compassion for others as God has compassion for us. The foreskin of our heart has been circumcised, and our heart of stone is replaced with a heart of flesh. We have substance and fortitude to endure hardship and adversity, and we have new weapons (spiritual weapons) to use in spiritual warfare. Praise be to our God.

We have victory in Christ because Christ is victorious. Our heart sings praises to the Lord as His glory is revealed through our deliverance. We rejoice because we have the joy of the Lord (which strengthens us) deep within our hearts. We rejoice because we know that Jesus is the light that guided us to victory. We rejoice because God chose to use our lives as examples of His strength, His might, His mercy, His compassion and His favor. Now we can dance and shout like never before because we know that God delivers right on time. In spite of ourselves and our own foolishness, the Lord brought us through and lifted us out of our troubles. We are living witnesses of what God did. Our lives have been transformed, and we have a more intimate relationship with the Father as a result of the process of our deliverance. Our spirit says, "Amen."

APPRECIATING THE PROCESS

The thing about climbing any mountain is that once you've reached the top, you have to come back down. After the travail, the triumph and the rejoicing, we have to come back down and face some of the same obstacles we encountered on our way up. The difference is, we know what the obstacles are and how to get around them. We can see them for what they really are, and just how much of a hindrance they were. When we come down from our spiritual high and look at what and how the Lord brought us through, we will rejoice even more. Our heart will be filled, and the glory of the Lord will come upon us.

Often, it's not until we come down from our spiritual high that we appreciate the process of our deliverance. There are many things we see after the triumph that we didn't see during the travail. We were too busy trying to endure to notice all the good that surrounded us. We forgot to stop and smell the lilies growing in the valley, and the sweet honeysuckle bushes amongst the thickets. We didn't notice them while we were trekking through the hard times, but they were there. Only after the travail and after the triumph are our eyes opened to see the beauty of what we missed in the process.

I was blessed to spend a few days in the Pocono Mountains with my sisters in Christ. As enjoyable as the weekend activities were and the release of every-day stress, it wasn't until the travel home that I was overtaken by an awe-inspiring moment of spiritual enlightenment. We were on our way home and enjoying a selection of gospel music as we drove downward through the mountain range. No one spoke a word as we traveled. Either we were just exhausted and didn't have anything to say, or we were all in a moment of deep pensive reflections.

In my own silence, I quietly sang along with the music as it echoed in my spirit like melodies from heaven. My heart embraced the splendorous sight of the mountains, and the Delaware River flowing at its base. Then in a moment of impulsiveness, I broke the silence with praises to God for the glory of His creation. "Look at that mountain! Look at the symmetry of the trees. Awesome! My God! Just look at that!" The music continued to penetrate my mind and spirit. Now and then, one of us grunted, "humph" in agreement with the words we heard.

As I looked up to view the sky, the clouds parted to expose the glory of the heavens. My eyes witnessed an extraordinary peep show when dark gray clouds incased in a silvery lining from the sun's reflection moved rapidly across the sky and brilliant orange and yellow rays of sunshine burst through. The sight of it caused me to whisper, "Awesome. Thank you Jesus." My soul began to praise the Lord inwardly as I controlled my excitement so as not to startle the driver. I couldn't help but smile, and even giggle as I thought about the might and power of God. How majestic is His creation.

There, in the midst of a silent praise, God gave me a 30-second flashback of my life. He showed me how the dark clouds of my life were always incased in the reflecting light of Jesus Christ. Jesus beautified every stormy and thunderous situation with the glory of His Holy Spirit. Every dark shadow cast upon my life was interrupted by bursts of God's glory illuminating the path of righteousness. The Lord spoke to my heart and reminded me that God blessed me with His goodness and gave me favor with man. He reminded me of the many times He delivered me when I was in trouble and in a state of spiritual decay. The Lord reminded me that His grace and favor were constantly with me in every situation. Softly I declared, "I am so blessed. God has given me so much favor. Thank you Lord for your favor."

Another parting of the clouds revealed a streak of light that penetrated the fog covering the top of the mountain range. It was as though the Lord put His finger through the mist and pointed it directly at me. God's love for me that endured over two thousand years reached down and touched me right then and there…in that moment. Trying to control my eyes from being consumed by tears and avoiding the inquiring minds of my sisters, I held my head down and squeezed them back inside. Silently the tears trickled down the side of my face.

Then I lost control and let out an exhaustive sigh. The driver glanced over at me and caught me fighting the tears. She politely said, "Okay, are you going to tell me about this?" Releasing another sigh, I squeezed out, "I am so blessed. I am highly favored by God." After that, I couldn't contain myself. Words of praise were in my throat, traveling to my palate, rolling on my tongue and pushing through my teeth. "God has given me so much favor. I have favor with God. I have favor with man. I am so special to the Lord, and I don't deserve it. Oh wretch that I am. I'm truly a sinner saved by grace. Why does He favor me so?"

The tears rolled down my face, and the spirit of the Lord filled me once again as I proclaimed to myself, "What a revelation!" What an awakening! Coming down from that mountain, God reminded me that He was with me all the time. Through thorns and thistles, stony ground, floods and strong winds, God preserved me with His grace and mercy, and He gave me favor. He extracted goodness out of the brier. He colored the bleakness of my life with shades of love. Truly God is majestic in all His ways. Then I thought to myself, why did God wait until I came down from the mountain to reveal Himself with such profundity? I thought God would have spoken to me when I was high on the mountain top enjoying the splendor of His creation. Instead, He chose to speak in His way and in His time.

To answer my question, the Lord impressed in my spirit this simple thought. When we're on the top of the mountain, we don't see the road that we traveled. Neither do we see the beauty of life growing out of the rocks (the joy of the Lord in adversity) because we're focused on the obstacles in our way. Sometimes we're so exhausted from climbing over adversity that when we're standing on top of our troubles, we get so caught up in the euphoria of the arrival that we forget to appreciate the process of going through the valley.

When we come down from the mountain top and walk back through the valley from which we were delivered, we will see that Jesus was with us in the valley all the time. Victory was already at hand because the Lord was always present. Psalm 23 lets us know that when we walk through the valley of the shadow of death (which most situations feel like), the Lord is right there taking care of us, guiding us, feeding us through His Word, helping us to overcome and pushing us towards our victory. He is just a prayer away. Our healing and deliverance is just a prayer away.

GOD IS EXALTED

Every time we go through a spiritual crisis and persevere, God is exalted. The Lord knows that we have hard times, and we often struggle to survive the wickedness in this world. He knows that there are times when we don't have that "grain of a mustard seed" faith that moves mountains. So He builds our faith by showing us that if we trust Him, He will help us to climb, drill through or go around every mountainous obstacle we encounter. The Lord builds us up and gives us the strength and fortitude we need to withstand suffering, adversity and persecution. God is exalted and the devil is defeated when we don't give up.

Every time we lift up the name of Jesus while we're enduring hard times, God is exalted. When we declare that the Lord has delivered us from the hands of the enemy, God is exalted. When we praise Him in the midst of our storm, God is exalted. When we rejoice regardless of how bad our situation may seem (or actually is), God is exalted. When God is exalted, He blesses His people. We are blessed because God is exalted in our lives. We have victory because God is victorious in our lives. Through His victory in us, the Lord draws others unto Himself. Praise the Lord!

Reflections

1. When you're going through hardships, suffering and persecution, do you stop, drop and pray, or do you wait until things get worse?

2. Do you praise God continually in the midst of your storm, or do you wait until you can see the break in the day before you offer Him your praise?

3. Prayer and praise are key to your victory. When you're climbing that stubborn mountain of a situation, prayer and praise will elevate you to a higher place in God. Don't give up, persevere! Victory is on the other side of your travail. You have over-coming power!

This is my prayer

"O clap your hands, all ye people, shout unto God with the voice of triumph. For the Lord most high is terrible; he is a great King over all the earth" (Psalm 47:1).

160

Lord, I'm so grateful for your overcoming power. I know that if I suffer with you, I will reign with you. I've suffered so much in such a short time, but I know that you were with me all the way. I know that in my travailing, I have overcome. I pray that you will accept my prayer and my praise for helping me to endure the process of my deliverance. I am so thankful that you extended your grace and mercy and gave me another chance to experience your love and compassion. I adore you, Master. You are my joy. You are my hope. You are my delight. You are my victory, and I will exalt your name forever. Hallelujah, and Amen!

Reverend Michele Taylor

SEVEN

CALLED, ANOINTED AND APPOINTED

(Destined to Serve)

"But we are bound to give thanks always to God for you, brethren beloved of the Lord, because God hath from the beginning chosen you to salvation through sanctification of the Spirit and belief of the truth: Whereunto He called you by our gospel, to the obtaining of the glory of our Lord Jesus Christ. Therefore, brethren, stand fast, and hold the traditions which ye have been taught, whether by word, or our epistle. Now our Lord Jesus Christ Himself, and God, even our Father, which hath loved us, and hath given us everlasting consolation and good hope through grace, comfort your hearts, and stablish you in every good word and work" (2 Thessalonians 2:13-17).

WHEN GOD CALLS OUR NAME

When God wants to get our attention, He calls us by our name. He knows us intimately and has a right to initiate a conversation with us. He doesn't have to wait for us to pray and evoke His presence. He initiates the encounter, and He expects us to rise up to the occasion and respond to His call. When God calls our name, He assures us that we are engaged in a direct and personal conversation with the Father. It is a one-on-one situation, and no one else is invited into the discussion. This is a very personal and intimate moment in our relationship with the Father that does not compare with any other.

When God calls our name, He intends to meet us in a special place that is Holy and sanctified. He will not enter into the midst of our sin to call us into the Holy of Holies. Rather, He calls us when we ourselves have entered into the inner courts of the sanctuary of our heart. He calls us when we have communicated to Him that we are willing to serve Him in some way. He calls us when our heart is pliable and our spirit conditioned to receive His voice. He calls us when we desire to have a more intimate relationship with the Father.

When God calls our name to usher us into the higher calling of ministry, He calls us with an urgency. He calls us with a clear purpose and direct intent. He calls us with precision and accuracy into the perfected and chiseled pathway we will walk in order to fulfill our detailed mission. He calls us out of the ordinary and into the extraordinary. He calls us out of the circumstantial and into the midst of our preordained destiny. He calls us out of the realm of impossible and translates us into the inevitable. He calls us out of things unseen into things foreseen.

KNOW WHO'S CALLING

Many have heard a voice calling them, but weren't sure about who it was that called. We need to know who's calling, God or man. The prophet Samuel was a young man when God called his name. When he first heard someone calling him, he went to Eli, the high priest, who was sleeping in an adjacent room. Certainly Eli had called upon Samuel in times past, and Samuel answered accordingly. Seemingly, this was no different, and Samuel immediately responded as he always did. However, Eli had not called Samuel, so he told him to go back to sleep.

God called Samuel a second time, and again Samuel went to Eli believing that Eli had need of his services. For a second time, Eli instructed Samuel to return to his sleep. Samuel heard his name called a third time and immediately arose to inquire of the priest's needs. Three times Samuel heard his name being called, and three times he responded, *"Here am I."* When Eli finally perceived that it was the Lord God who called Samuel, he instructed Samuel to answer, *"Speak Lord for thy servant heareth"* (I Samuel 3:9). In obedience, Samuel did as he was instructed. The scripture lets us know that inasmuch as Samuel ministered *"unto the Lord before Eli"* (I Samuel 3:1), he did not yet know the voice of the Lord. Therefore, when God called his name, he did not know that it was the Lord who summoned him.

God Himself stood next to Samuel and called him one more time. Samuel responded according to Eli's instructions, *"Speak Lord for thy servant heareth."* When Samuel acknowledged the presence of the Lord who called him, God proceeded to speak with Samuel intimately concerning the house of Eli. From that day forward, Samuel was established as a prophet of Israel to deliver the message of salvation and reconciliation. Not one word spoken from his mouth went unfulfilled.

We who are called by God to preach the gospel must know that it's God who calls us. The devil does not call us to deliver the message of salvation and redemption, but that of confusion and destruction. If we hear in our spirit a voice that tells us to destroy the handiwork of God, we know it's not God's voice. The sheep of the Lord know the Shepherd's voice, and will respond. The voice of the Lord is distinct and clear in its purpose and intent for righteousness. His voice echoes into the soul of those who desire to be united with the Father through redemption. His voice speaks to man's need for reconciliation, and the restoration of the intimacy of our fellowship with our Father.

HOW LONG?

Each one of us has a very different, distinct and unique personality, characteristics and character flaws. As such, God deals with us in a way that speaks directly to our individuality and differences. The timeframe for which the Lord waited for me to respond to His calling is not the same as the timeframe for which He waited (or waits) for your response. How long God waits for us to respond is according to His own good pleasure.

I was a little girl when the Lord impressed in my heart the desire to preach. I thought it was a game when my sister and I played church in our basement. We sang the songs of Zion, clapped our hands and acted just like what we saw others do in the church. When it came time for the Word of God, we both took turns preaching to each other and our pretend congregation. We preached so well, that we were moved to shout! (That's what we saw in our church, so that's what we did.) How were we to know that an innocent child's play was a part of God preparing our heart to receive the calling to ministry?

Growing up, I remember feeling that one day I would stand before millions of people and preach. Though I wasn't saved and had no immediate plans to be saved, I was drawn in by the Word. I recall in high school having an admiration and respect for a friend who accepted the call to ministry. One evening, I went with his girlfriend to hear him preach. I was so taken in by the preaching that I wanted to get behind the pulpit and preach right along with him. I heard the voice of God calling me many times over the years, but it wasn't until I accepted Jesus Christ into my life that the call became real.

I was 21 years of age when God called me into the ministry. I heard Him when He called, but I chose to ignore His voice. I wanted to sing, not preach. Even though the Lord blessed my voice, singing wasn't the ministry for which I was preordained. I was sitting in service one day when I distinctly heard the Lord instruct me to preach and teach the gospel. I responded to the teaching ministry and ignored the preaching ministry. Teaching was not a problem because I enjoyed teaching. Teaching Sunday School was a challenge, but not a struggle. Teaching teenagers was a challenge, but not a struggle. Teaching adults in various educational and academic settings was a challenge, but not a struggle. I was quite comfortable and satisfied with teaching the Gospel, but that wasn't all that the Lord required of me. In spite of myself, God waited patiently and with longsuffering while I ignored His instructions to preach.

Time kept moving forward, and I thought I had gotten away from my destiny. I thought I maneuvered my way out of the calling. At a time when I least expected (the mountain-top experience), the Lord reminded me that He called me to preach the gospel of Jesus Christ; "Go and tell." (Herein began the days of a serious struggle.) I said, "Okay Lord," as an appeasement, and I went back into a deep spiritual slumber. I kept saying, "I hear you Lord, but I'm not ready." The alarm was going off in my spirit, and I kept hitting the snooze button.

I must tell you, I experienced so much turmoil in the years that I ignored the Lord that had I tried to climb Mt. Everest, it would have been a much easier task. I was fighting a fight I could not win. When I finally said, "Yes Lord," with conviction and total surrender, the preaching anointing rose up within me, and the struggle was over. God's patience and long suffering endured the grief I gave to the Holy Spirit, and my own self-induced suffering. All I had to do was surrender to the *will* of God when He first told me to preach the gospel. All I had to do was say, "Yes" and act upon my commitment. In doing so, I really would have saved myself from certain needless tribulation.

The Lord took the years of my disobedience and turned them into an opportunity to prepare me for the intricacies of servitude required for the ministry. He taught me the difference between my concept of time and His. He showed me what it means to have patience by His own patience and longsuffering with me. The Lord showed me that He has the final say over my destiny, and that which He put in me (the spiritual and ministry gifts) will eventually have to come out in order to fulfill the purpose for which they were given. Herein, the Lord showed me that He was constantly molding and shaping me for His divine purpose regardless of my own actions and decisions.

SAY "YES"

When we say "Yes" to the call to ministry, we consciously acknowledge and activate our faith, and we commit ourselves to work. We have faith that God will help us to do what He called us to do, and we have an expectation to work because "ministry" is an action word that requires physical labor. We trust God to instruct us every step of the way; and we have faith that whatever the Lord would have us to do, He will prepare and equip us with the knowledge, wisdom, education and experience we need to be effective. We trust that our heavenly Father will never leave us comfortless or without hope when disappointments and adversities come. We know that the Lord will lead and guide us by His Holy Spirit as we endeavor to do His *will* and serve His people.

By saying, "Yes Lord," we are motivated to get busy for God! We become active participants in God's divine plan for the healing and restoration of nations. When we say, "Yes," to the ministry, we're saying yes to be used by God for the working of miracles to save the unsaved, to heal those in need of healing, to comfort those that are comfortless, to mend the broken-hearted, to give heart (courage) to the heartless, and to deliver from bondage those that are captive in the foreign lands of Satan's prisons. We are inspired to compel others to come into the safety of the ark through the covenant with Jesus Christ. He is our mercy seat in Heaven, and our righteous Savior in God's plan of redemption.

By saying, "Yes Lord," we fulfill our hunger and thirst for righteousness. We become motivated to study the Word of God with the purpose of acquiring the knowledge, understanding and wisdom that enables us to be more effective in our witnessing. Our heart's desire is to be endowed with God's anointing so that we can impart His message of love; as exemplified through the life of Jesus Christ, with conviction and transforming power. To say, "Yes Lord," means that we willingly accept the responsibility of the ministry and submit ourselves into the skillful hands of the master potter to mold, shape and reshape us at His *will*.

THE RESPONSIBILITY OF THE CALLED

The call to ministry is also a call to a level of responsibility that we have never known before. Honestly speaking, when I gained a little understanding of what it was God called me to do and the responsibility of the calling, I

171

shuttered deep within my soul and quickly withdrew. That's not an uncommon reaction (so I learned from talking with other ministers). There's a feeling of humility and unworthiness that overtakes the called (at least there ought to be) that causes us to revere and pull back. The thought that God would even consider us as useable is quite humbling.

When I considered all that I had done that did not reflect God's spirit working in me, I found it difficult to believe that the Father called me to such great levels of responsibility. Souls were at stake (even my own), and I felt unworthy—even untrustworthy. I didn't trust myself and wondered how it was that God trusted me with a task of such magnitude. I decided within myself that I wasn't capable and equipped to do the job. I concluded that surely someone else was better qualified, and I started to name a few people that came to mind. I tried to rationalize, intellectualize and analyze my resistance in relation to my understanding of the new responsibilities I faced. In the process, I prophesied myself right out of the divine *will* of God, and my pseudo-humility turned to disobedience.

I attempted to negotiate with the Lord what I would and would not do. I found more excuses than a handful as to why I couldn't accept the responsibilities of the ministry. I didn't have time! I didn't have money (it takes money to do ministry). My seminary education was limited. I didn't like talking in front of people (even though I won several oratorical contests and studied speech extensively in college). Neither did I look the part. (I wasn't into wearing big frilly hats.) The excuses went on and on. In reality, I didn't want the responsibility. God forbid I should make a mistake! What if I led someone the wrong way, or gave advise that caused them to make a bad decision?

The Lord saw right through my excuses, fears, doubts, insecurities and inadequacies and gave me another chance to accept the responsibility of the ministry. The Holy Spirit spoke to my heart and counteracted my excuses. When I got over myself and accepted the fact that ministry comes with a great deal of responsibility and God trusted me to be responsible, I was humbled even more. (What if someone accepts salvation because we accept a little responsibility? Hallelujah!)

BY APPOINTMENT ONLY

The Called are Anointed and Appointed by God. One of the reasons why some of us have had (or are having) problems with accepting the responsibilities of ministry is because we are not clear about what ministry we are called to. Many are called to ministry, but few are chosen for specific ministries. We are not all chosen to the ministry of deliverance and exorcism (though we can all rebuke the devil). We are not all chosen to pastor (though many are called to lead). We are not all chosen as evangelist (though we are all called to witness). *"...and He gave to some, apostles; and some, prophets; and some, evangelists; and some, pastors and teachers" (Ephesians 4:11).*

The word "some" implies "partial." Only part of the Body of Christ have been chosen to these ministries. As such, they (we) are given a measure of grace to walk in their (our) higher calling and to accept the responsibilities that go along with the calling. They (we) are appointed by God and anointed by His Holy Spirit to do a work that can only be done by the one to whom it was appointed. When we know and understand the ministry we have been anointed for and appointed to, we can work more effectively in fulfilling our calling. God anoints our potential and causes the ministry to prosper. Because the ministry prospers (spiritually), souls are won for Christ, and God is glorified.

A word of caution! Some of us have been appointed to positions in ministry by our pastor and have mistaken this appointment as God's calling without ever going to God to verify the appointment as His divine *will* and purpose. Indeed pastors are given the wisdom and discernment to know the gifts and callings of their parishioners. However, the pastor's appointment to ministry positions are not always by divine revelation or in line with God's calling. Appointments to the ministry can sometimes be motivated by personal reasons and hidden agendas to obtain material and financial gain, power, prestige and recognition. Sometimes people are appointed to the ministry because no one else is available to fill the position, political reasons, nepotism, to appease financial supporters or to avoid the character assassination of those in leadership.

The true calling to ministry is by God's appointment only; not by the pastor, or someone who "just loves the way you speak." God's appointment is divinely purposed, spiritually motivated and eternally secured. When God appoints us to ministry, He also anoints us. In His anointing, we can reach our full potential in the ministry for which we are called. We are called to serve. We are anointed to serve, by the mercies of God. We are appointed to serve. We are destined to serve. God expects us to serve. It is His *will* that we serve. It is an honor and a privilege to serve. Therefore, we ought to serve with gladness and gratitude. (Fulfill your destiny and accept the Higher Calling of God to serve.)

SURRENDER TO GOD

The Lord has chosen you to minister to His beloved people; those that are saved, and those that are yet to be saved. You have experienced God's love through His delivering power. You know what God can do because of what He's done for you. Every situation you've ever been in and come through is a testament to God's glory in your life. You're the one God called to be a witness. You're the one God set free, opened doors that were once shut, created jobs for when there were no jobs, provided sustenance for your family when you were laid off from work. You're the one who prayed and God delivered you from some serious problems that almost consumed you emotionally, mentally and physically. You're the one who said, "Lord if you bless me...if you get me out of this mess, again...if you just do it for me one more time, I'll do whatever you want me to do. Lord, if you need someone, here am I. Send me." Beloved, it's time to honor your vow!

This is not the time to run from your calling. The seal of the Holy Spirit on your life is a guarantee that God's eminence dwells within you and reigns supreme. You feel His spirit nudging you and prompting you to surrender. This is the moment of truth (so to speak). God is asking you to surrender your all to Him; your heart and soul, your body, spirit and your mind. With your whole heart, accept the call to ministry, and the responsibility that comes with it. I cannot tell you that life will be easier. In fact, it may become more trying. However, to surrender your *will* to God's *will* to fulfill this high office of service is a great honor. To serve the almighty God is worth every trial and tribulation you will ever experience. Don't reject your calling. Accept it and be blessed.

What a blessing it is to share God's Word. What a blessing it is to submit to the moving of the Holy Spirit and to operate in God's anointing. Oh, what a joy it is to walk in your calling! If you know you are called by God to the ministry, Surrender. Say, "Yes Lord. Here am I. Send me." Honor your vow.

Reflections

1.   Do you know what aspect of ministry you are called to?

2.   Are you doing the ministry you were called to do, or are you trying hard to avoid it at all cost?

3.   The Lord has selected you for a particular ministry for a particular reason. He knows who you are, what you've done and what you're going to do. God has anointed and appointed you to a specific ministry. Therefore He will prepare you and equip you with the necessary tools to do the job. In spite of what you may think and feel, you are capable. The question is, are you willing? Though you may feel unworthy, the Holy Spirit in you makes you worthy. Now it is up to you to walk worthy of the Lord in your calling. Glorify God by fulfilling your calling to ministry.

This is my prayer

"The spirit of the Lord God is upon me; because the Lord hath anointed me to preach good tidings unto the meek; he hath sent me to bind up the brokenhearted, to proclaim liberty to the captives, and the opening of the prison to them that are bound; To proclaim the acceptable year of the Lord, and the day of vengeance of our God; to comfort all that mourn; To appoint unto them that mourn in Zion, to give unto them beauty for ashes, that oil of joy for mourning, the garment of praise for the spirit of heaviness, that they might be called trees of righteousness, the planting of the Lord, that he might be glorified" (Isaiah 61:1-3).

Lord, I thank you. I am so grateful that you called me to the ministry. Though the task may be a difficult one, I surrender to your *will*, and I accept the responsibility. Help me, Father, to do what you have appointed me to do. Release your anointing in me and use me to your glory. Do a work in me, Lord, and perfect the things concerning me. Fulfill your destiny in me. Here am I, Lord. Send me, I'll go. Hallelujah!

EIGHT

IN A WORD
(Obey)

"But this thing commanded I them, saying, Obey my voice, and I will be your God, and ye shall be my people: and walk ye in all the ways that I have commanded you, that it may be well unto you" (Jeremiah 7:23).

"Then they that feareth the Lord spake often one to another, and the Lord heard it, and a book of remembrance was written before him for them that feared the Lord, and that thought upon his name. And they shall be mine, saith the Lord of hosts, in that day when I make up my jewels; and I will spare them, as a man spareth his own son that serveth him. Then shall ye return, and discern between the righteous and the wicked, between him that serveth God and him that serveth him not" (Malachi:3:16-18)

.

I CONFESS

There are so many things the Lord instructed me to do that I have not done. Some things, the season is over and will not return again. Other things, I am moving on slowly, but moving nevertheless. In my slothfulness and outright disobedience, God continues to extend His grace and mercy towards me. His grace is sufficient to cover my arrogance, stubbornness, faint-heartedness and lack of commitment. His longsuffering shows me just how patient He really is, and how His love for me covers my sins, rebellion and rejection of His *will*. I am so grateful that the Lord looks at me through the redeeming veil of the blood of Jesus Christ.

Writing this book is an act of obedience. Much of its content addresses what I've learned as a result of my own disobedience and the process of learning to be obedient. Nearly ten years ago, the Lord instructed me to write my testimony. I was excited at first because I wanted to share what the Lord had done for me. However, when I thought about what to write, fear gripped me. I was afraid of what "they" would say. I was afraid to expose my shortcomings and things I had done that weren't so "pretty," or "godly." I trembled to think of my past haunting my present and running over into my future. I didn't want to open old wounds and address unresolved issues that were buried deep within me. I didn't want to relive the trauma, drama and emotions that filled my past.

I admit to the difficulty of revisiting my past in order to share with you in detail how the Lord healed and delivered me. I wrestled with what I would share and what I would withhold. I cried intensely as I typed certain passages because the Holy Spirit prompted me to release many safe guarded feelings and hurt. Several times, I walked away from the computer while I was in the middle of writing sentences that evoked a moment of intense emotionalism. I stopped writing for months—thinking I would avoid having to deal with my feelings, and that I could escape the task of sharing painful experiences. I even questioned God, "Lord do you really want me to write this?"

I know the Lord loved me through the difficult passages and reassured me of His *will* as I continued to journey through the process of being molded and shaped, baked and broken, then molded and shaped again. I went through the fire of refinement, and I'm yet being refined.

I confess! Ten years ago, I would have written with anger and vengeance rather than with love, respect and forgiveness. Though the Lord delivered me from various situations, trials, tribulations, persecution and church hurt, there

was a great deal of anger, hatred and bitterness
that needed to be cleaned out of my heart and my
spirit. When the Lord healed my heart and
renewed my spirit, He gave me love and
forgiveness for people (Christians and non-
Christians) that hurt me so badly. He restored my
soul and blessed me to have a greater love for His
people.

Time and Process were key factors in God's
making me over. Time heals all wounds, and
Process is our teacher. The combination of these
two elements puts us in the place where we can
begin to overcome. I know that I have overcome
because when I encounter similar situations to
what I've already gone through, the way I handle
them now is quite different than how I did before.
In revisiting the past, I found out that the pain
didn't hurt the same as it did then; I wasn't angry
anymore, and I had even forgotten what it was I
was angry about in the first place. My bitterness
was made sweet, and my arrogance turned to
meekness. Situations that once caused me to
dislike certain people in the church didn't seem to
matter anymore. I found myself extending mercy
and compassion instead of hate.

I confess! I was convicted when I looked back
and found that there were still some areas that
needed work. There were still a few people I
needed to forgive, and a few emotions I needed to
let go of. How long can we be angry at people for

what they did to us? How long will we hold on to the hurt and pain? How long will we be unforgiving? Letting go is necessary for our healing, and to overcome. We know that we are healed and have overcome when we are able to let go of the past, learn from it and move forward into victory.

HEAR AND OBEY

When God speaks, we ought to listen. The Lord is constantly speaking to us through His Word, nature and our conscious and subconscious mind. We hear God's instructions when we read His Word. We hear God speaking to us through the very elements of the earth telling us to prepare for the coming of the Lord Jesus. We hear God speaking to our conscious and subconscious mind when He gives us instructions on a daily basis. Regardless of the vehicle the Lord chooses to speak through, we need to listen and adhere.

All too often, we've ignored God. In a quiet whisper, He told us to bless someone financially or to walk away from a situation or to intervene in another situation, and we didn't. The Holy Spirit may have prompted us to do something very specific, and we chose not to, or we put it off until we felt the time was right. We intellectualize, rationalize and analyze God's instructions and find every logical and practical reason not to do what is in our spirit to do. As a result of our disobedience, we miss our blessing and cause others to miss their's as well.

We disobey until we learn to obey. More often than not, learning to obey God comes from our experience of disobedience. We endure suffering, chastisement and many unnecessary hard times because of our disobedience. We went through situations that were a direct result of our disobedience. Many of our tests and trials were a direct result of our disobedience. Many of our decisions were based on acts of disobedience; and like the domino effect, one act of disobedience without seeing the immediate consequences made it easy to disobey again.

Every act of disobedience has a consequence. Whether we see it now or later, the consequences are inevitable. Isn't it better to obey God and be blessed than to disobey and reap the consequences? It's a simple matter. When the Lord tells us to do something, we ought to just do it!

Reverend Michele Taylor

DISOBEDIENCE WITHIN THE BODY

Individually, we all have a purpose in the Body of Christ. We are all essential members joined together by the hands of the Master. Each part of the Body of Christ has a specific function that when joined together exemplifies the wholeness of God in perfect working order. When each member functions at maximum capacity, the Church Body is more effective. When one member is spiritually weak or cripple, we all suffer.

Our disobedience within the Body of Christ is crippling and causes an imbalance. Someone has to take up the slack for what we are not doing, or are incapable of doing at the time. Which means that someone will be called out of their function and put into another function in order to compensate for the weakened member. The effectiveness of the church may be compromised as a result of our individual and corporate acts of disobedience.

Many Christians are functioning outside of their calling and spiritual office because of our disobedience, and the church is suffering as a result. Some church communities are not prospering spiritually and financially because the leaders (pastors, overseers, trustees, lay leaders, etc.) have not done what God told them to do.

The consequences of their/our disobedience is quite evident in the local church, the Church Body and the communities we serve. (God forgive us.)

OBEDIENCE REQUIRES DISCIPLINE

No one said obedience is easy. Most of us don't like to be told what to do; not even when it's the Lord who gives the instructions. It is in our human nature to rebel against authority and instruction because we are the sons and daughters of Adam. However, as born again believers, our old ways are made new.

Obey God: Putting all things into perspective, we have to let go of some of our old habits and take on the ways of holiness. Holiness requires that we discipline our tongue, our thoughts, our flesh and our actions. When we've gained control over these areas, we will be able to hear God speaking to us more clearly, and we will respond more readily. We are servants of the Master; bondsmen of Jesus Christ. As such we are given instructions through the Word of God as to what we can do to keep our flesh under subjection. By following Christ as our greatest example, we can learn to walk in holiness with temperance and grace.

Obey leadership: We are commanded to obey our leaders and follow them as they follow Christ. It takes discipline not to rise up against leadership when they themselves are not being obedient to God. Whether or not we agree with our leaders, the Holy Spirit compels us to exercise self-discipline. The Holy Spirit teaches us to control our tongue from speaking out against our leaders in anger and with malice. He teaches us to submit to those who have rule over us in respect to their position and office. It isn't always easy to do what we're told to do; and we don't always understand why we are told to do certain things, but in our obedience, we learn submission and humility. God called our leaders into positions of authority, and He is molding them the same as He is molding us. I've learned the hard way that our leaders are yet in the hands of the Master, and what He does with them in the molding and shaping process is His business. When we submit ourselves to the authority of leadership and honor our leaders in their respective office, God will bless us.

Obey sound doctrine: We have to discipline ourselves to follow sound doctrine and not be moved by every wind of doctrine. It takes discipline to stand fast and not be moved every time a new doctrinal movement enters the Church. If we are not steadfast and unmovable, we could get caught up and swept up with the movement. To endure sound doctrine and not go with whatever comes our way because it looks and sounds good takes self-control and the knowledge of the Word of God. Which means that we have to discipline ourselves to study the Word of God. Knowing the scriptures and applying them to our lives will help us to stand for righteousness and not buckle under the pressure of wickedness.

OBEDIENCE MAKES US TRUSTWORTHY

Our obedience to God proves us to be trustworthy. God can trust us to do the right thing with what He's given us. He trusts us with the gifts, talents and skills He's imparted into us. He knows that we won't bury our talents or misuse and abuse our spiritual gifts. God knows that we will use the resources for which we are stewards over to care for the poor and destitute, and to bless His people. When we are faithful over a few things, God makes us ruler over many things, and we can enter into the joy of the Lord. *"His Lord said unto him, Well done, good and faithful servant; thou has been faithful over a few things. I will make thee ruler over many things: enter thou into the joy of thy Lord" (Matthew 25:23).* The Lord knows

189

that we will not seek vainglory for ourselves. Rather, we will lift up the name of Jesus so that the Father will be glorified.

God trusts us to rise up out of our disobedience to do His *will*. He has confidence in our love for Him and our desire to be the servants He called us to be. The Lord searches our heart and knows our intent. So He's patient with us because He knows exactly what we are going to do and why. He gives us time to get ourselves together and realign ourselves with His *will*. In the meantime, the Lord extends His grace and His mercy so that we are covered during the process. God's grace is truly sufficient, and His mercy endures forever!

THE BLESSING OF OBEDIENCE

The blessing of obedience is our wellness in God. *"But this thing commanded I them, saying, Obey my voice, and I will be your God, and ye shall be my people: and walk ye in all the ways that I have commanded you, that it may be well unto you"* *(Jeremiah 7:23).* (Hallelujah!)

I desire wellness in my soul. Therefore, I strive to obey God. My spirit is uneasy when I have not done what God requires of me; I cannot rest, there is no peace. I don't enjoy struggling with inner turmoil when I have ignored God's instructions. It is not a good feeling. My subconscious wrestles with my conscious, and my spirit wars against my flesh every time I'm disobedient. However, when I have obeyed the voice of the Lord, and have done what He has commanded me to do, I am free. My spirit is free, and I have peace of mind. It is well with my soul.

The blessing of obedience is freedom. The weight is off me. The burden is made light. I am no longer bound (captive) by the fear of what might happen if I just do what God told me to do. I can see the miracles released in others; the healing, and the deliverance. When I've done what the Lord requires me to do, I can walk in the blessings of the liberty of Christ—even though persecution may follow. To be persecuted for Christ's sake is a blessing. The blessing of obedience is to be called a child of God by God. We are children of the most high God! We are royalty—heirs to the throne. We are His, and none of His will be lost. This is His promise. Therefore, let us obey God and be blessed. Amen.

Reflections

1. What did God tell you to do that you have not yet done? What are you going to do now?

2. God is merciful and forgiving. In our disobedience (even rebellion), God can and will forgive us when we ask Him. Ask the Lord to forgive you for your acts of disobedience, and submit to doing His *will*.

3. Obedience to God brings liberty and peace. When you've done what He asks you to do, you will be free, and you will find peace. Walk in His peace.

4. My soul desire is to be used by God. I pray that He will find me trustworthy so that He can use me.

This is my prayer:

"As for me, this is my covenant with them, saith the Lord; My spirit that is upon thee, and my words which I have put in thy mouth, shall not depart out of

thy mouth, nor out of the mouth of thy seed, nor out of the mouth of thy seed's seed, saith the Lord, from henceforth and forever" (Isaiah 59:21).

Your Word is in my mouth, Oh Lord, and your spirit is upon me. I desire to obey your Word; and, I desire to do that which you commanded me to do. As Christ obeyed you, even unto death, help me to be obedient that it might be well with my soul. Let your covenant stand in me, and I will stand in thee. Forgive me when I have fallen short, and restore me unto obedience. To thee, Oh Lord, be all the glory, majesty and power. In the name of Jesus, Amen.

Reverend Michele Taylor

EPILOGUE

All praises to the God of my salvation. Blessed is the name of the Lord. It is my joy to have shared just a few of my experiences with you during my own process of being molded and shaped by the Lord. Even in preparing this book, God is yet refining me for His service. I've endured much persecution, many trials and great tribulation during the three years for which this work was constructed. I've been attacked spiritually on every hand with opposition from loved ones, jealousy from not-so-loved ones, afflictions in my body and the unspeakable thorns in my side. Yet, by God's mercy and divine *will* declared in the heavens, He has allowed the completion of this project for His own glory.

The Making of You is truly an act of obedience. The deliberation behind every word scribed was for the sole purpose of honoring God with the use of the gifts He imparted into my spirit. I have the eternal peace of God within me because I pushed forward, endured the attacks from the adversary and did what the Lord instructed me to do. My spirit is free because I have obeyed the Lord's voice to "tell the truth." In this, He has shown me that I, too, have reached a new level of spiritual maturity. Yet, I am still in the process of being shaped and reshaped as the Lord continues to mold me into the woman of God He purposed me to be. There is much more refinement I must go through on my journey to fulfilling God's *will* for my life, and my preordained destiny for service. Which means that at any given moment, I could be back on the potter's wheel.

I pray that you have found something in the pages presented that will help you to make it to the next level of your destiny. You have to go through; you have to get through, and you have to tell someone about your journey as God carried you through. Your life is not your own; it belongs to God. He has a divine plan for every aspect of your life, and He will enact His plan as He chooses. He is making you according to His *will* and good pleasure. Hold on to your faith; hold on to The Faith, and allow the Lord to do a work in you that will glorify Him. May God's peace be with you always, through the comforts of the Holy Spirit, in the process of *The Making of You.*
Reverend Michele Taylor

About the Author

Reverend Michele Taylor resides in Queens, New York, where she and her husband share an outreach and teaching ministry. She has a BA in Sociology, an MA in Social Policy, certificates in Christian Ministry, Leadership Development, Training Administration and various secular and Christian educational forums. Her experience as a church administrator, Christian educator, program and curriculum developer, retreat and conference coordinator and leadership trainer has given her many insights to Christian maturity and spiritual development. She has a heart for teaching adult learners, women's ministries and social welfare. Reverend Taylor's passion for writing inspired the creation of Taylor House Publications. Her love for travel, nature, the ministry and God's people is reflected in every aspect of her writing.

Printed in the United States
20085LVS00001B/169-231

9 781410 724427